mont-blanc

second edition 2004

written and edited by
Michael Kayson & Isobel Rostron

Qanuk Publishing & Design Ltd
www.snowmole.com

the snowmole guide to **chamonix mont-blanc**
first published in the UK in 2003 by winter press
copyright © winter press 2003
ISBN 0-9545739-1-9

the snowmole guide to **chamonix mont-blanc**
second edition 2004

published by Qanuk Publishing & Design Ltd
45 Mysore Road London SW11 5RY

copyright © Qanuk Publishing & Design Ltd 2004
maps © Qanuk Publishing & Design Ltd 2004
artwork © oliver brodrick-ward 2003

printed by Craftprint, Singapore

ISBN 0-9545739-3-5

A catalogue record of this book is available from the British Library.

snowmole does not accept any advertising or payment, and the guides are written free from any bias.

The contents of this book are believed correct at the time of printing. As things can change, errors or omissions may occur. The publishers and authors can accept no responsibility for any loss, injury or inconvenience sustained by anybody using information or comment contained in this guide.

contents

how to use the guide

How much you enjoy your winter holiday depends on a variety of things. Some you cannot influence - you can't guarantee sunshine, good snow, or your flight landing on time... but most things should be within your control. With the majority of ski holidays lasting just a week or less, you don't want to waste time trying to find a good restaurant, or struggling with an overgrown piste map. The snowmole guides are designed with 2 purposes in mind: to save you time by providing essential information on the operation of the resort, and to help you to make the most of your time by giving insight into every aspect of your stay.

The guide is not intended to be read from cover to cover. After the introduction to the resort, the guide is split into 4 distinct sections - getting started, the skiing, the resort and the a-z - so you can dip into the information you need when you need it. Some information will be useful to you beforehand, some while you are in resort and some while you are on the mountain.

getting started   deals with the basics: how to get to the resort, how to get around once you're there, and your options when buying your lift pass, renting equipment and booking lessons or mountain guides.

the skiing   gives an overview of the mountains and the ski area, information on the off-piste, and a breakdown for beginners, intermediates, experts, boarders and non-skiers. The ski domain has been divided into digestible chunks and for each there is a detailed description of the pistes and lifts.

the resort   covers the best of the rest of your holiday: a series of reviews on where to eat, where to play, what to do when skiing isn't an option, facilities for children and tips for seasonnaires. Those places that in our opinion deserve a lengthier review are written as a 'feature'.

the a-z   comprises a list of tour operators, a directory of contact details (telephone numbers and website addresses) and information from accidents to weather, a glossary of terms used in this guide and in skiing in general, and an index to help navigate your way around the guide.

how to use the maps

The guide also features a number of maps, designed and produced specifically for snowmole. While the information they contain is as accurate as possible, some omissions have been made for the sake of clarity.

route maps   show the journey to the resort from the UK, or from relevant airports or the roads within the area surrounding the resort.

resort maps   for the resort as a whole (showing pedestrianised zones, main buildings, car parks, train lines, and road names) and individual maps showing by type the places we review.

ski maps   each individual area has its own contoured map. These show details such as the lifts, pistes and mountain restaurants. The contours have been mapped to fit an A6 page - few ski areas are perfect rectangles. They are accurate only in relation to the pistes they depict and should not be used for navigation. Pistes are shown only in their approximate path - to make the maps as user-friendly as possible some twists and turns have been omitted. The ski maps are grouped together at the back of the book to make them easy to find and refer to - even with gloves on. There is an overview map on the inside back cover that shows the entire ski domain and how the individual ski maps fit together. The back cover has a flap, which is useful as a page marker for the individual ski maps. In the chapter on the skiing the overview map is reproduced in miniature alongside the descriptions of the individual sectors.

explanation of icons

review headers

← price rating

relevant icons →

map details: page number, grid reference & map cutout showing type and number reference

name

☎ 0479 055578
🕐 7:30-10:30am, 4pm-10:30am
✕ traditional savoyarde

p107
b4

basic details

☎ - telephone number
📠 - fax number
@ - email address
W^3 - website address
🛏 - number of beds
🖃 - office address
🕐 - opening hours
✕ - food type

ski school

⛷ - ski lessons
🏂 - snowboard lessons
🎿 - child-specific lessons
♿ - disabled skiing
⛷ - specialist courses
G - guides available

hotel

🛍 - on-site rental store
🚌 - shuttle bus

others

✕ - food available
♫ - live music
📺 - tv
🔌 - internet station(s)
🍸 - bar
• - terrace

resort maps

buildings

ℹ - tourist office
lp - lift pass office
PO - post office
🛒 - supermarket
🎬 - cinema
✝ - church

travel specific

P - parking
🅿 - covered parking
ⓑ - bus stop
🚌 - route specific bus stop

commerce colour coding

■ - restaurant (local cuisine)
■ - restaurant
□ - cafe
■ - take-away
■ - bar
■ - nightclub
■ - hotel

route maps

 - train line & station

 - main road & town

 - country borders

 - motorway & town

 - airport

graphic design by
Ranuk Publishing & Design Ltd

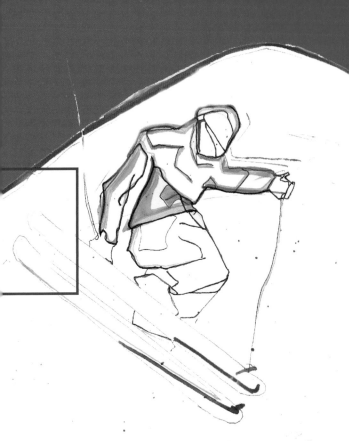

introducing chamonix

overview

Almost everything about Chamonix is different from a typical ski resort. It is renowned for being the extreme skiing capital of the world - and indeed much of the steepest, narrowest and most dangerous skiing in the Alps can be found in the valley - but there is far more to Chamonix than that. While the surrounding mountains make it a Mecca for climbers and mountaineers as well as skiers and snowboarders, there is plenty of on- and off-snow activity for those less inclined to danger. Perhaps the truest thing that can be said is that people do not go there to be seen - they go there to have been. Chamonix has few pretensions, and the fashion is more for Dakine backpacks than for Prada ski outfits. While it is

expensive it does not even approach Val d'Isère or Courchevel prices, and while you can stay in a luxury 4* hotel you can also stay in a €12/night dormitory. There are some excellent restaurants and the most diverse après in the Alps, but people go there to ski.

That said, Chamonix is not for everyone. The skiing is not gentle, the view from the town is as intimidating as it is spectacular, there is no ski-in/ski-out accommodation, the valley's ski areas are separate and the only way between them is by road...

but Chamonix has a charm quite unlike anywhere else. Whether you are drinking coffee by the river, practising turns on the pistes, or skiing the Vallée Blanche, there is something compelling about being under the gaze of Mont Blanc. And people either like it or they don't.

Chamonix is much larger than a typical resort, and is a fully functional town in its own right. It is effectively divided into two: the centre of town - a bustling blend of bars, restaurants, shops and hotels; and Chamonix Sud, which has its own distinct flavour but which is predominantly made up of mid-grade hotels and apartment blocks. The town is not really an attractive place, and with its popularity increasing every year the little old world charm that remains is being tightly squeezed by commercial progress. In contrast, the narrow valley, through which the River Arve flows, is surprisingly spacious and outstandingly beautiful. Only Chamonix and

10

Argentière are well developed, and very little of the mountain area is tainted by lifts and pistes.

And who goes to Chamonix? In short, everyone. In high season the tourist population is over a third English - so if you're looking for an authentic French getaway, Chamonix is the not the place you'll find it. Along with the English, it is most popular with Swedes and other Scandinavians, though its worldwide renown also draws Russians, Americans, and a surprising number of non-skiing Asian tourists. It is a popular weekend destination for the French, and with its proximity to 2 borders a lot of day-trippers come over from Italy and Switzerland.

11

For a ski resort, Chamonix has a mind-boggling range of accommodation - over 70 hotels along with countless chalets, apartments, gîtes and dormitories. At most times of year there is likely to be something available somewhere, but if you know where you want to stay it's best to book early.

> **snapshot**
>
> **highs...**
> some of the best skiing in the Alps
> the Vallée Blanche
> large and diverse town
> 1 hour from Geneva airport
> can be done cheaply
>
> **and lows**
> ski areas not linked
> limited gentle skiing
> high on-piste speed
> very busy town with lots of traffic
> logistically difficult for mixed ability groups

Thanks to the size of the town, there is enough diversity in the after-ski department to cater for every price range and pretty much every taste. The always-busy après scene is traditionally centred on the Rue des Moulins, a cobbled pedestrian street which offers 5 bars, 4 restaurants, 2 cafés and a night club - but the rest of the town has an almost limitless choice of crowded sports bars, welcoming local pubs, riverside cafés, or whatever takes your fancy. You won't be bored.

The same is true of eating out. There is enough demand to support endless Savoyarde incarnations, traditional French restaurants that include the Michelin starred Albert Première, and food from every corner of the globe - Sushi, Tex-Mex, Indian, Chinese... the list is as long as the mountains are high. You can spend €5 or €50 on your meal depending on the preference of your palate or the generosity of your wallet.

Chamonix's best - and worst - aspect is its skiing. Its reputation for steep, unforgiving runs is well deserved, and there is enough on-piste challenge to provide a workout for even the most advanced skiers. There is also plenty of intermediate level skiing, enormous off-piste opportunity and ample provision for beginners. By name the 4 areas are Le Brévent, La Flégère, Les Grands Montets, and Le Tour. Only Le Brévent and La Flégère are linked, so if you are staying in Chamonix the only way to Les Grands Montets and Le Tour is by road. This is the root of most of the complaints about the skiing - to catch the first lift at Le Tour you can't just roll out of bed at 8:30am and crawl to the gondola station, because it's about 10kms away.

12

Similarly, to ski the Vallée Blanche you will have to do a fair amount of queuing for the cable car, and to ski it without the crowds you will have to get up very early indeed - but all of Chamonix is much as with Heinz tomato ketchup. Good things come to those who wait.

And if you prefer to take the stairs rather than wait for the lift, Chamonix is also a great place - perhaps *the* great place - for ski touring. Only a tiny percentage of the surrounding mountains have ever seen a piste basher, and the overwhelming majority of skiers - even in Chamonix - never stray out of sight of the markers. This leaves a huge amount of terrain untainted and untouched, and hence available to the ski mountaineer.

Predicting the weather in the mountains is always difficult, and in Chamonix it's tricky even from the bedroom window. While the valley sits below a bank of cloud, the surrounding peaks can be basking in sunshine.

temperatures

It's fairly easy to generalise temperatures - December and January are usually the coldest months, with things warming up gradually through February, March and April. When you are in resort, don't be fooled by appearances - it will often be colder when there is a cloudless, blue sky than when snow is falling.

13

Temperatures can range from -15°C at ground level on the coldest days to as high as 20°C later on in the season when the sun is shining.

snowfall

When and how much snow falls varies from year to year, but general trends do emerge. Snow falls sporadically on the upper slopes throughout the year. Snow cannons along the line of the

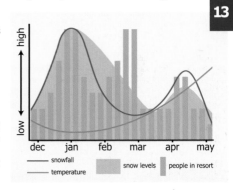

— snowfall
— temperature
snow levels
people in resort

Bochard lift make Les Grands Montets the first area to open, usually in late November. By Christmas, there is usually enough snow cover to open everything except the runs down to Chamonix and Les Praz. The snow normally continues to fall through January and historically snow levels peak in February, in time for the busiest weeks. As temperatures rise in March, the snow levels drop again. Late season snow is common, though the falls are less sustained and because of the higher temperatures, what falls doesn't last as long on the upper slopes, and lower down barely settles at all.

volume of people in resort

As Chamonix has the largest seasonnaire population in the Alps, the town is never quiet - though the slopes are still significantly less busy in low season. Like most other major resorts, it is busy over Christmas and New Year and very busy for 2 weeks in February during the English and French school half-terms.

Ski resorts are as varied as DNA. But what makes Chamonix Chamonix? To have a quintessential time...

be in awe

As you come out of the tunnel past Servoz and turn the corner into the valley, you are confronted by a wall of rock so steep and high that it almost blocks out the light. As you get closer, the Aiguille du Midi swings into view, then the imposing jagged ridgeline leading towards Les Grands Montets. If you've never been to Chamonix before, it will take your breath away. If you heart isn't beating faster by this time, you should see a doctor.

stand in the queues

Chamonix is a big place, but not big enough for the number of people that go there. No matter what you want to do, you will have to wait for someone else to do it first. There are queues for the buses, queues for the lifts (almost all of them!), queues to get to the bar, queues in the supermarket, queues in the ski school offices... but this gives you time to reflect on where you are, and where you would be if you weren't there. Better the Grands Montets cable car than the London Underground.

tilt at windmills

Chamonix is a place for lofty romanticism, but if you fancy a break from your quixotic side there are more achievable ideals to be found on Cham's original row of windmills. At the north end of the modern town, the Rue des Moulins is these days a cobbled pedestrian street which offers perhaps the highest concentration of commerce anywhere in the Alps. Haircuts, clothes, coffee, dinner, beer and clubbing are all crammed into a 50 yard stretch. Hi-ho, Sancho!

take a tour

Chamonix has a lot of history, and lot of impressive things to see. There are a number of ways to deal with this - read one of the books, wander round the museum, cruise the streets with Dr Jivago, or go on a guided tour. Non-skiers can book onto one through the tourist office, but to find out about the true culture of the mountains your guide should be a mountain guide, and your tour should be on skis. Pluck up the courage, do something different. You won't regret it.

keep with the fashion

At work, men wear suits and women wear trousers. On the beach, men wear baggy swimming shorts and women wear bikinis. At weddings, men wear morning suits and women wear hats. In Chamonix, regardless of your gender, what you need is a scruffy pair of thermals, a rope, a Suunto watch and an ice axe.

walk the arête

Perhaps the most famous hundred yards in Chamonix, and for many people the most frightening thing about skiing the Vallée Blanche. From the Aiguille du Midi you can only get there by making your wobbly way down a narrow path that on a normal day will be icy, slippery, and jammed full of people. It is enough to put off quite a few people, especially children. But once you've done it, you've done it - the first of many things about skiing the Vallée Blanche that make great photo opportunities and even better fireside stories.

What's the best way to get down the arête? Carefully.

never leave

If you look out of the window at work, what do you see? Offices? Open the window at home, what do you hear? Cars? Put things in perspective. You probably work 8 hours a day, 5 days a week, about 50 weeks a year. That's 2000 hours. You probably ski 6 hours a day, 6 days a week, 1 week a year. That's 36 hours.

That's more than 55 hours of work for every hour of skiing. Chamonix more than anywhere else in the Alps will make you think about that ratio.

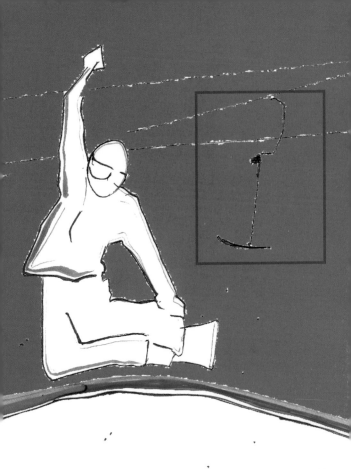

getting started

Once you know you want to go to Chamonix, you need to decide how you want to get there. Traditionally, most skiing holidays are booked though travel agents or tour operators, but with the advent of cheap flights, DIY holidays are becoming more popular. There are pros and cons to both.

18 package

The theory behind package holidays is that all you should have to think about is getting from the top of the slopes to the bottom. The core of every package deal is convenience - though it comes wrapped in all kinds of paper. Ski companies fall into 2 types: large mainstream operators, and smaller more specialist ones. The mainstream brand offers ready-made holidays, where everything is already planned and you take it or leave it. Trips with smaller companies can be more expensive, but tend to be more flexible and many tailor the trip to your exact requirements. Alternatively, if you don't want to be restricted to one operator, a travel agent will have access to a selection of holidays offered by several companies.

Mainstream companies only run week-long trips, from Saturday to Saturday or Sunday to Sunday - giving you 6 days on the slopes and 7 nights in (or on) the town. They charter their own **flights** - making the holiday cheaper - but you have little option as to when or from where you travel. Smaller ski companies give you greater choice - many specialise in long weekends for the 'money-rich, time-poor' market, with departures on Thursday evenings and returns on Monday evenings. This gives you 4 days skiing for 2 days off work... but the real advantage is their use of scheduled flights, so you can pick the airport, airline, and when you travel.

With a mainstream company, your **transfer** journey to resort will be by coach, with others who have booked through the same company. You may have to wait for other flights, and on the way there may be stop-offs in other resorts or at other accommodation before your own. Because you're travelling at the weekend the journey tends to take longer. With a smaller company you may transfer by coach, minibus, taxi, or car depending on how much you've paid and the size of your group. And if you arrive mid-week, the transfers tend to be quicker.

What your **accommodation** is depends entirely on whom you book with. Different companies have deals with different hotels, some specialise in chalets, some operate in specific resorts... the limiting factor is what's in the brochure - though if you want to stay in a particular hotel, a more specialist company may try to organise it for you.

In **resort** some companies offer a drop-off and pick-up service from the lifts, which is a huge advantage in sprawling Chamonix. But the main benefit of a package holiday is the resort rep. From the moment you arrive to the moment you leave, there is someone whose job it is to ensure your holiday goes smoothly... or that's the theory. More than likely your rep will sort out lift passes and equipment rental. Some will organise evening activities and be available for a short period every day to answer questions. Most are supported by an in situ manager who deals with more serious issues. The more you pay for your holiday, the better your rep should be. The best are service-oriented French speakers... but it is difficult to recruit hard-working, intelligent, bilingual people to work for next to nothing. If you want to know what - or who - to expect, ask when you book.

DIY

If you DIY, you have more control over the kind of holiday you take and what you pay. But as you have to make all the arrangements, you'll need more time to plan the trip.

Both traditional (BA, Swiss) and budget airlines (bmibaby, Easyjet) schedule regular **flights** to Geneva - the nearest major airport to Chamonix. You can fly from all major UK airports, though the cheapest flights are normally from London, and the earlier you book the cheaper it will be. The airlines accept reservations for the upcoming winter from around June or July. Some

chartered airlines such as Monarch or Thomas Cook may also have a limited number of seats for sale. For **transfers** to your resort ➜ getting there. If you don't want to fly, the excellent European motorway system makes **driving** to the Alps surprisingly easy. Getting there by **train** is also an option.

On a DIY trip the choice of **accommodation** is endless - you are not restricted by brochures or company deals... however the easiest way to book a chalet or an apartment is through a company or website offering accommodation only, such as Interhome or ifyouski.com. You can liaise with the owners directly if you can find their details, but this is often difficult. For hotels you might be able to get a discount off the published price by contacting them directly. For more information on hotels, chalets and apartments ➜ accommodation.

In **resort** is perhaps where the difference between DIY and package is most noticeable. There is no rep on hand so you have to buy your own lift pass, organise your own equipment rental... but this can have its pluses: you can be sure that you get exactly the right type of pass and you can choose which rental shop you use.

19

getting there

One of Chamonix's many attractions is how easy it is to reach: you can wake up in London and be on the slopes of Le Brévent by lunchtime. Below are details of the various ways of getting yourself to the mountains. All contact details for the transport listed can be found in the directory.

20 overland

The most common starting place for any journey by **car** to the Alps is Calais. You can reach Calais from the UK by the **eurotunnel** or **ferry**. It is then just under 600 miles (a little over 900km) from Calais to Chamonix, and the journey can be done in 10 hours or less. The journey from Calais takes you east of Paris, through Reims to the mustard town of Dijon (about two-thirds of the way if you want to make an overnight stop along the way). The final stretch of the journey takes you past the south tip of Lake Geneva (though you never enter Switzerland) on a two-lane motorway (known as the *Autoroute Blanche*). If you are travelling on a Saturday you can expect traffic and delays on this part of the journey. Chamonix Mont-Blanc is clearly signed and you barely need to make a turn, so it is very difficult to go wrong.

There are 4 *péage* (toll) stops on the route south through France, for which you collect a ticket as you enter the motorway and hand it in as you leave. Expect to pay around €50 in total - you can pay with cash or by credit card.

If the scenery around Lake Geneva tempts you into taking a detour through Switzerland, you will have to buy a *vignette*, a windscreen sticker which acts like a motorway pass (the equivalent of the French péage). It costs around €25, and is good for the duration of the year in which you buy it. If you haven't got one before you get there, you can buy one at the border control.

There are 2 alternatives to the standard **ferry** crossing to Calais. The first is with Norfolkline to Dunkerque - often quieter (and less prone to lorry strikes!) than the Calais services. The second is SpeedFerries.com - a new fast ferry service to Boulogne. SpeedFerries sells tickets on a similar basis to the budget airlines - the earlier you buy, the less you pay.

Eurolines run a direct **coach** service between London and Chamonix 3 times a week in each direction. The journey takes about 19 hours and you travel overnight.

The classic way to reach the Alps from the UK by **train** is on the **snowtrain** or the **eurostar overnight** service. In theory travelling this way gives you more time in resort - 8 days instead of the usual 6. It's an excellent service if you live in London and are skiing in the 3 Vallées or the Espace Killy, but it doesn't work out so well for a skiing holiday in Chamonix. For both these

21

fly-drive p.23

london
dover
folkestone
calais
dunkirk
boulogne
arras
lille
A26
st. quentin
A26
A4
reims
châlons-en champagne
A26
troyes
A5
langres
A31
dijon
chalon
A39
auxerre
paris
rouen
chartres
orléans
le mans
tours
rennes
nantes
poitiers
limoges
bordeaux
toulouse
clermont-ferrand
st. etienne
lyon
valence
grenoble
geneva
lausanne
bern
luzern
zurich
basel
nice
monte-carlo
turin
genoa
milan
verona
venice
bologna
stuttgart
frankfurt
cologne
rotterdam
brussels
luxembourg
munich
innsbruck
salzburg
prague

NL
B
L
F
D
CZ
A
CH
I

copyright qanuk 2004

services the only stops in the Alps are Moûtiers, Aime and Bourg-St. Maurice - all some distance from Chamonix. There isn't a direct train service to Chamonix from any of these stations, so you have to complete your journey by car, which takes at least 2 hours. If you are still undeterred, be sure to book well ahead, as the services become full months in advance.

If you're intent on travelling by train, the **TGV** (the French intercity service) takes you more directly to Chamonix - or at least to Annecy, from where you take a SNCF train on the Saint Gervais/Le Fayet-Vallorcine line, which stops in Chamonix. There is a direct service for Annecy from the Gare de Lyon and the Gare d'Austerlitz in Paris. The total journey from Paris to Annecy takes approximately 5 hours. To get to Paris, you can either fly or take the Eurostar.

by air

The nearest airport to Chamonix is Geneva. You can fly to Geneva from any major airport in England (➥ planning your trip).

transfers

Once you have safely landed in Geneva, you can get to Chamonix in one of 5 ways.

As Chamonix is only 60 miles (90kms) from Geneva, getting there by **car** is a real option. You can hire a car at

Geneva airport by booking over the phone, on the internet, or when you arrive at the airport. Your car will have the necessary equipment required to legally travel on French roads such as an emergency triangle but you will need to specifically request snow chains and a roof box if you want them. From the airport follow the green signs to France - you will reach customs within about 15 minutes. Once you are in France, join the A40 heading south-east and follow signs to Chamonix Mont-Blanc. The 2 péage stops on the motorway (the Autoroute Blanche) cost about €3 each.

There is no direct **train** service between Geneva airport and Chamonix - you have go to Annecy or Annemasse and change, and to get to either of those you have to go to Geneva mainline station and change. If you are competent at finding the right platforms, the journey will take you around 2 hours.

public buses run every day between Geneva airport and the train station in Chamonix. There are 4 services each way on weekdays and 5 each way at weekends. The service is much like the National Express, and the journey takes just over 2 hours.

If you don't want to have to worry about driving yourself or sharing your personal space, there are a number of companies which run **private minibus**

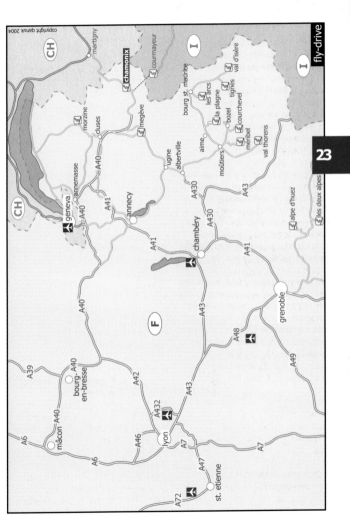

23

transfers from the airport direct to your accommodation. Services vary from a simple pick up and drop off to the provision of welcome packs and food and even champagne during your trip and are significantly less expensive than in a private taxi. There are a number of services that operate in the Alps including ATS, Alp Line, Mountain Transfers and Alpine Cab. All of them pick up from Geneva airport and take online bookings, either via email or direct through the relevant website. ATS run shuttles from Geneva, as well as private transfers while Alpine Cab is the luxury option. Bordercross is a Chamonix-based service who run private transfers for up to 8 people.

You can always take a **taxi** though the privilege of doing so isn't cheap - a one-way trip from Geneva airport will cost you approximately €150. Or you can take a **helicopter** with Chamonix Mont Blanc Hélicoptères if you want to arrive in real style.

24

Getting to Chamonix is the easy bit. Getting around once you're there can be quite an effort, and is for some people the most disappointing side of a Chamonix ski holiday. It isn't very complicated, but getting from one end of the valley to the other can be very time consuming - and if you aren't careful about choosing your accommodation, just negotiating your way into town can take a chunk out of your day.

chamonix valley

With no traffic it's about a 15 minute journey from Chamonix to Le Tour - but with a lot of cars on the road it can take upwards of 45 minutes. Unless your hotel or tour operator provides transport, your options are either to take the bus or to drive.

Given the enormous number of people that use the **chamonix bus** every day, it is remarkably efficient. You rarely have to wait for more than 10 or 15 minutes for a bus to turn up, and at peak times they come more frequently - though of course they are far busier. There are a variety of services, most of which loop around the ski areas, but some of which simply shuttle to Chamonix's satellite towns - so make sure you check the destination on the front of the bus. The service is free with the ChamSki lift pass (➥ lift passes). There are also **night buses** between Chamonix and Argentière - one bus runs every hour in each direction

snapshot

from chamonix by road
chamonix valley
argentière 10 mins
les praz 5 mins
le tour 15 mins

other resorts
courmayeur (italy) 20 mins
les houches 10 mins
megève 30 mins
morzine 45 mins
verbier (switzerland) 1 hour

25

between 8pm-11:45pm. By far the easiest way around the valley is by **car** - no waiting, no queuing, more than a square foot of personal space during the journey... if you have your own transport all you have to worry about is the traffic, which can be considerable at peak times - Chamonix is subject to a rush hour in much the same way as a busy English town. There are plenty of pay car parks in Chamonix (as marked on the town map). There is also parking along many of the roads in town, pay & display during the day but free over lunchtime (the gendarmerie who dish out the tickets are on siesta between 12pm and 2:30pm) and in the evenings as well as free parking (for 1 day) past the hotel Gustavia.

For specific information on getting to and parking at each ski area ➥ the relevant entries in the skiing.

chamonix town

Chamonix is big for a ski resort, but by
no means so big that you need to drive
around town - it takes about 20 minutes
to walk from one end to the other. The
town centre is largely pedestrianised,
and while there is some traffic through
the middle it is very slow moving. Le
Brévent and the Aiguille du Midi
are within walking range of town,
and you can get to La Flégère on
the cable car liaison from Le
Brévent - but Les Grands Montets and
Le Tour are only accessible by road.

26

Though restaurants, bars, shops and so
on are well spread throughout the town,
in general the areas are divided as
follows: the Place Balmat (town e3),
Place Sassure (e3) and the pedestrian
cobbles of the Rue des Moulins (e3/4)
are home to bars, cafés and
restaurants; the main shopping is split
between the Avenue Michel Croz (e3)
and the long stretch from the Rue
Joseph Vallot (f4) to the end of the Rue
du Docteur Paccard (c4). The best spot
to catch a bus is on the Avenue du
Mont Blanc (f3) at the end of the Rue
des Moulins, and the best place to get
off for the town centre is at the end of
the Rue Whymper (e2). In Chamonix
Sud the main drag is the Avenue de
l'Aiguille du Midi (b/c3), and the main
bus stop is next to the Bowling Pub
(a3/4).

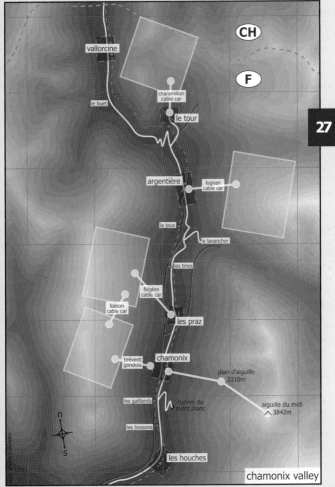

27

vallorcine

CH

F

le buet

charamillon
cable car

le tour

argentière

lognan
cable car

la joux

le lavancher

les tines

flégère
cable car

liaison
cable car

les praz

brévent
gondola

chamonix

plan d'aiguille
2310m

les gaillands

tunnel du
mont blanc

aiguille du midi
3842m

les bossons

n

s

les houches

chamonix valley

accommodation

At the end of the day on the slopes, you probably won't mind where you rest your head. But when planning your holiday, you might want to put more thought into where you stay. This is particularly relevant in the Chamonix valley where there is accommodation of every kind available from Les Houches at one extreme to Le Tour at the other - and anywhere in between.

Accommodation - hotels, apartments, b&bs and chalets - can be booked through the tourist office, either by telephone (t 0450 532333) or over the internet (i reservation.chamonix.com).

hotels

Chamonix's hotel accommodation ranges from exquisite luxury to down and dirty dormitories. Anything and everything is available. Per night you can spend as much as €800 or as little as €12. Service and facilities vary accordingly - often the more you pay, the more formal the hotel will be, from the restaurant (if there is one) to the service throughout - at the top end, the Albert Première boasts the valley's only Michelin starred restaurant, and at the other end of the scale the Ski Station gîte charges a supplement every time you take a shower.

Choosing a hotel in Chamonix can be quite a complicated business - given the spread out nature of the ski areas you need to work out where your priorities lie. Do you want to be close to a bus stop? Close to the shops? Close to the slopes? Close to the Aiguille du Midi cable car? Whatever you plump for, you can at least be assured that you'll have a stunning view out of the window. Because of how spread out the skiing is, no hotel can be ideally placed for everything. If you are planning to take a car, be aware that many hotels around the centre of town have little or no parking space.

specifics

Some hotels will only accept week-long **reservations**, especially if you are booking a long time in advance. Outside of low season, last-minute bookings are likely to be relatively difficult to make, but the number of beds in the valley means you are likely to find something somewhere - if you are determined enough to spend a day by the phone. Many hotels have a deal with a specific **rental shop** - they will advise you of this when you check in. The majority of the hotels have a number of rental shops within easy walking distance. Every front-of-house employee will speak **english**, so unless you have a quibble with a cleaning lady you will be able to survive with no French at all. But hotels are where you will notice a difference if you can speak in French. Staff are more likely to be more sympathetic to questions (or complaints) if you make the effort to communicate with them in their language. In France the number of stars a hotel has is directly connected to its

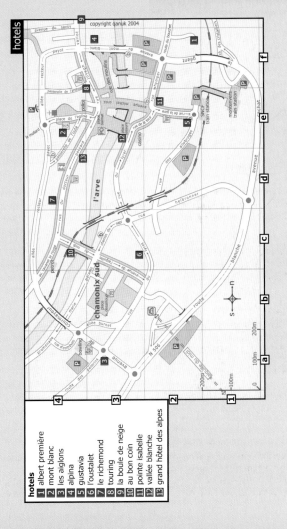

hotels
1. albert première
2. mont blanc
3. les aiglons
4. alpina
5. gustavia
6. l'oustalet
7. le richemond
8. touring
9. la boule de neige
10. au bon coin
11. pointe isabelle
12. vallée blanche
13. grand hôtel des alpes

accommodation

facilities. Things like room size and whether there is a lift dictate how many stars are awarded. Where the rating system can be misleading is in the divide between 2* and 3*. Often a room in a 3* hotel will not be noticeably different to a much cheaper room in a hotel with 1 less star. Nonetheless the 4* hotels are generally the most comfortable and have the widest range of facilities. Though getting around the Chamonix valley can be a bit of a drag, very few hotels provide a private **shuttle** bus. It would be entirely impractical to try to cater for the whims of every guest - the few hotels that do offer this service face a logistical problem.

prices
The price ranges are approximate figures for a double room per night in high season, including tax but not service.
luxury over €150
mid-range €80-150
budget €30-80
shoestring under €30
All hotels accept most credit cards. Thanks to the high seasonnaire population and the thriving summer season, there is plenty of low cost accommodation dotted around the valley for those on a real shoestring - this bracket is unique to the Chamonix guide, and is intended for those working with a next-to-negative bank balance. There are reviews for hotels of note in Chamonix (grouped into the 4 price

---

snapshot
for...
cheap as chips - touring
families - hermitage paccard
good food - eden
liveliness - gustavia
location, location - alpina
peace & quiet - bois prin
luxury - albert première
nouveau luxury - grand hôtel des alpes

brackets), along with a brief list of alternative options and reviews for a few of the hotels in Argentière.

<< luxury >>

albert première****

☎ 0450 530509
📞 0450 559548
@ infos@hammeaualbert.fr
𝒲³ hammeaualbert.fr
🛏 42 (b&b, ½, full)

p29
f2

The French hotel rating system only goes to 4* - the Albert Première is a strong argument for a 5th. It offers every conceivable luxury, a swimming pool with indoor and outdoor sections, a horse-drawn cart to carry you through the snow to the town, 12 palatial hammeau 'rooms' with - amongst other things - their own fireplaces and 2 restaurants - the wonderful Maison Carrier and the Michelin starred Albert Première (which is difficult to get into unless you're a hotel guest). It oozes formality, and is very expensive, but it is the summit of professionalism and if you can afford it you should consider nowhere else.

mont blanc****

☎ 0450 530564
📞 0450 558944
@ mont-blanc@chamonixhotels.com
𝒲³ chamonixhotels.com
🛏 39 (b&b, ½, full)

p29
e4

A beautiful, spacious and excellently located hotel - at the foot of the hill that leads to the Brévent, next to the tourist office and across the road from the Maison de la Montagne. It has a large reception and lounge area, a very formal feeling bar which regularly hosts live musicians, the highly regarded Matalan restaurant, intelligently professional service... and while it doesn't quite have the prestige of the Albert Première (and some of the bedrooms could do with an overhaul), it wants for very little and is more convenient for the centre of town.

31

auberge du bois prin****

☎ 0450 531843
📞 0450 535150
@ boisprin@relaischateaux.fr
𝒲³ boisprin.com
🛏 18 (b&b, ½, full)

town **e4**

Run by the same family as the Albert Première, the Bois Prin has the same excellent service and provision of every luxury, but it is out of town in a quiet and spacious location. It is high enough that technically you could ski back to the door - but only if you can find your own way,

accommodation

eden**

☎ 0450 531843
📠 0450 535150
@ relax@hoteledenchamonix.com
W³ hoteleden-chamonix.com
🛏 13 (b&b, ½)

In the small town of Les Praz, the Eden is one of the best-kept secrets in the valley. It is a 1 minute walk to the Les Praz bus stop, and a 2 minute walk to the Flégère base station and the Ravanel & co rental shop. With the liaison cable car that links La Flégère to Le Brévent, being 5 minutes drive from the Chamonix town centre is only limiting if you are concerned about your après schedule - Les Praz is not a lively place. But for anyone who wants to avoid the rough and tumble of the bars and clubs (or anyone with their own transport/money for a taxi), staying at the English-run Eden guarantees you a homely welcome that you would be hard pushed to match anywhere else.

Though its lack of luxuries mean that by the French system it only qualifies as a 2*, the rooms are more than comfortable enough to ease away any aches you may have picked up during the day (or night). The restaurant (→ eating out) is one of the best in the valley, the bar doesn't close until the last person leaves... if you are looking for good value, simple comfort, outstanding food, and impeccable and personal service, the Eden is the place to be.

as there's no piste. It is another splendid example of French attention to detail - and its smaller scale makes it feel more personal. A fine restaurant and bar mean this is a place you may find it difficult to leave after a day's skiing.

grand hôtel des alpes****

☎ 0450 553780
📞 0450 558850
@ info@grandhoteldesalpes.com
W³ grandhoteldesalpes.com
🛏 30 (b&b, ½, full)

p29
d4

A new hotel right in the centre of town, the Grand Hotel des Alpes is aimed at the new wave of big spending, luxury seeking holidaymakers who choose Chamonix for its cosmopolitan feel and convenience rather than extreme skiing. It lives up to its name with marbled bathrooms, a spacious foyer and a swimming pool... though the biggest attraction is the chalet-style Ancienne Tour suite that is bigger than some actual chalets. You can't fault the location, and some rooms are not as pricey as you might expect.

<< mid-range >>

gustavia***

☎ 0450 530031
📞 0450 558639
@ hotel@hotel-gustavia.com
W³ hotel-gustavia.com
🛏 47 (b&b, ½, full)

p29
e2

The perfect location if you want busy après-ski with your holiday - the Gustavia boasts Chambre Neuf as one of its rooms and has both Elevation 1904 and Goophy's (➜ après-ski & nightlife) just across the road. The Chamonix bus stops on the doorstep, and the SNCF train station is across the road - this is not the place for refined luxury, but if you want comfort coupled with absolute convenience, it is on offer here. The clientele is largely English and Scandinavian, and is mostly (but not exclusively) on the young side. The Gustavia also has a resident masseur, a piano room, a terrace (part of Chambre Neuf), very friendly service, and all of Chamonix just outside the front door.

33

hermitage-paccard***

☎ 0450 531387
📞 0450 559814
@ info@hermitage-paccard.com
W³ hotelhermitagechamonix.com
🛏 30 (b&b, ½, full)

accommodation

A large chalet-style hotel just outside the centre of the town. It has its own grounds, and therefore more space than some of the hotels in town, including an outdoor play area for children. Rooms are both modern and traditionally styled, and facilities include the excellent Crémerie du Paccard restaurant (→ eating out), a gym, a sauna and a games room. Its downside is that it's a 5 minute walk to the town centre - the pay-off being that in the other direction it is only a 5 minute walk to the MBC (→ après-ski & nightlife). All in all it is airy and spacious, friendly and welcoming, and somewhat quieter than the hotels in town - and though it is somewhat more expensive than most 3*, it is well worth spending the extra money.

alpina***

☎ 0450 534777
📞 0450 559899
@ alpina@chamonixhotels.com
W³ chamonixhotels.com
🛏 136 (b&b, ½, full)

If what's important is where you are rather than who you're with, the Alpina is your place. It is very, very large, across the road from the Rue des Moulins and just off the main bus route through town - so you will never have to walk far to get anywhere. You are unlikely to find personal service, but the Alpina has facilities that some smaller hotels in the same price range don't have - a games room, children's entertainment, and a gym, jacuzzi and sauna - and thanks to a clever architect all the balconies feel private. The glass-walled Restaurant 4810 on top of the hotel isn't bad, though it is not as good as its view.

savoyarde***

☎ 0450 530077
📞 0450 558682
@ lasavoyarde@wanadoo.fr
W³ lasavoyarde.com
🛏 14 (b&b, ½, full)

A small and cosy hotel in the perfect place to ski Le Brévent - at ski boot mph it is literally a 1 minute walk from the gondola station, and, for beginners, the Savoy learners' slope. The Savoyarde is run by the Carrier family (of Bois Prin and Albert Première fame), and has the same attention to detail in a slightly less expensive and less formal environment. Compared to larger hotels what it lacks in luxury it gains in personal service - the only drawback is that the restaurant won't keep you interested for more than a couple of nights and while getting down the hill to town isn't difficult, getting back up to bed might well be. The nearest rental shop is across the road from Le Brévent lift station.

les aiglons***

☎ 0450 559093
📞 0450 535108
@ info@aiglons.com
W³ aiglons.com
🛏 56 (b&b, ½, full)

A large block of a hotel right next to the Cham Sud main bus stop. The Aiglons is far nicer inside than out, the rooms are large and very comfortable, and it has the gym, sauna, and restaurant you would expect from a large hotel. It's a fair walk to the town centre but if you want the Jekyll and l'Impossible (→ après-ski & nightlife and eating out respectively), the Bowling pub, easy access to Cham Sud and the Chamonix bus, there's nowhere better. Staying in the Aiglons is definitely a choice about where in town you want to be.

l'oustalet***

☎ 0450 555499
📞 0450 555498
@ infos@hotel-oustalet.com
W³ hotel-oustalet.com April & 2006
🛏 15 (b&b)

A beautiful mid-size chalet hotel in an excellent location. Situated on the edge

of Cham Sud, 2 minutes walk from the Aiguille du Midi cable car and the same from the centre of town - but not on a main route to either, and so never noisy. It only offers b&b accommodation, but its proximity to everything means that dining out is never a hassle, and there is a hotel bar for pre-dinner drinks. It is very comfortable throughout, and many rooms have balconies facing Mont Blanc.

35

<< budget >>

touring**

☎ 0450 535918
📞 0450 539771
@ info@hoteltouring-chamonix.com
W³ hoteltouring-chamonix.com
🛏 24 (b&b)

If you can find the pokey entrance on Rue Joseph Vallot and don't mind the shoebox corridors, the Touring will give you a cheap bed in the middle of town. It is English-run, and so hassle-free, though if you are driving, be aware that you won't be able to park anywhere near the hotel.

richemond**

☎ 0450 530885
📞 0450 559169
@ richemond@wanadoo.fr
W³ richemond.fr
🛏 53 (b&b, ½)

accommodation

The perfect place for those who don't want to pay for luxury but don't want to sacrifice comfort and service. The town centre is just outside the front door. Rooms are surprisingly spacious and the 2* rating is due only to the few facilities. The Richemond provides a comfortable bed in much the same vein as the Eden and the Aiguille du Midi hotels but with the added bonus that it is easy to get to.

36

that you would miss out on if you stay further up the valley. And you needn't miss out on the Chamonix experience - though it is a 5 minute drive out of the centre they provide a free shuttle to get you around. This can leave you a little reliant on the needs and desires of your fellow guests, but if you don't mind that - or you have a car - this is one of the best mid-range option in the valley.

<< shoestring >>

l'aiguille du midi**

☎ 0450 538065
📞 0450 559369
@ hotel.aiguille@telepost.fr
W³ hotel-aiguilledumidi.com
🛏 40 (b&b, ½)

Much like the Eden in Les Praz, the Aiguille du Midi is a splendid and very English-friendly hotel that has a lovely restaurant and provides everything you need at a decent price. It's south of the town, in Les Bossons, and at the foot of the Glacier de Bossons - a stunning view

vagabond

☎ 0450 531543
📞 0450 536821
@ gitevagabond@hotmail.com
W³ gitevagabond.com
🛏 9 (b&b, ½)

The Vagabond is true slumming - it sleeps 38 but there are certainly not 38 rooms. There is 1 private (and very charming) room right at the top, but otherwise you're back at boarding school. If you make friends easily and

don't mind sharing your living and sleeping space with people you've never met before, the Vagabond allows you to stay a night in Chamonix for the price of a pitcher of beer. It is English-run, and has a dark, cramped and excellent bar where you can get to know your next bunk neighbours.

☎ 0450 530173
📷 -
@ -
w³ -
🛏 11 (b&b)

A little further out than some options, the Aiguille Verte is much the same kind of offering. Very basic, very cheap, and entirely what you want if you want everything except for a high price tag. No gym, no spa, no anything much except for beds and showers. But if you need something to do, look out of the window. It's only 5 minutes from town, it's right next to a bus stop... and what else do you need?

esor## accommodation

la boule de neige*

p29
f/g3
9

☎ 0450 530448
📷 0450 559109
@ -
w³ -
🛏 9 (b&b)

The Snowball is a little way out of the town centre, but is close to 2 rental shops and is only a short walk from the Alpina bus stop which gives you good access to the ski areas. In addition, if you are a beginner it is only a very short walk to the bottom of the Savoy learners' slope. Inside the hotel, the pleasing wooden décor gives it a homely feel, and the bar and restaurant aim their service at the hotel customers - cheap and cheerful.

37

and the rest

Where to start? There are any number of alternatives in and out of town from the 4* Jeu de Paume (t 0450 540376, i jeudepaumechamonix.com) in Le Lavancher to the 0* Ski Station by Le Brévent gondola. The tourist office will provide you with a comprehensive list which you can work through alphabetically, chronologically or however you like. For a more focused approach read on. Other options **in town** include the 3* Vallée Blanche (t 0450 530450, i vallee-blanche.com), the 2* Au Bon Coin (t 0450 531567) and the 2* Pointe Isabelle (t 0450 531287, i pointe-isabelle.com). **out of town** towards Les Gaillands is the small

accommodation

and friendly La Chaumière (t 0450 531325, i hotelchaumierechamonix.com) run by mountain guides. On the way to Les Praz (home of La Flégère) is L'Arveyron (t 0450 531829, i hotel-arveyron.com) and in Les Praz you can stay at the 2* Les Lanchers (t 0450 534719, i hotel-lanchers-chamonix.com) or the 3* Labrador (t 0450 559009, i hotel-labrador.com), home to the Cabane restaurant. Further up the valley by the Jeu de Paume in Le Lavancher is the 3* Beausoleil (t 0450 540078, i hotelbeausoleilchamonix.com). Or if you want to pretend that you're staying in somewhere with the same **ski in/ski out** convenience as the 3 Vallées, the L'Olympique (t 0450 540104) next to the Le Tour gondola is at least the former.

argentière

In the shadow of Les Grands Montets the small town of Argentière could be considered a resort in its own right. While Chamonix is attractive for its diversity and cosmopolitan feel, a decision to stay in Argentière is normally made by people whose priority is a certain kind of skiing. While the choice of accommodation in Chamonix is more than most people need, if 50 restaurants, 30 bars and a constant throng of people sounds less attractive to you than being able to walk to the base of the Lognan cable car, it may be worth choosing somewhere to stay a little further up the valley. Though this

small road-side resort doesn't have the range of hotels that Chamonix offers - there's a lot less choice and nothing at all in the luxury bracket - there is plenty of comfort to be had, much of which won't damage your wallet too badly. And the big attraction is that you're never far from your nearest lift station. The base stations for Les Grands Montets is a mere stroll away from all the hotels - about as "ski-in/ski-out" as you'll get in the valley. And if the bumps of Les Grands Montets get a bit tiresome there are bus stops dotted throughout the town. Otherwise the **specifics** are the same as for Chamonix.

les grands montets***

		p119	16
		b2	

☎ 0450 540666
📞 0450 540542
@ info@hotel-grands-montets.com
ʷ³ hotel-grands-montets.com
🛏 48 (b&b, ½)

The easiest way to catch the first lift, and the most luxurious of Argentière's hotels. The chalet-style building is just a couple of minutes walk from the Lognan cable car, and the centre of Argentière is about 5 minutes away. All rooms have homely wooden décor, and there is a beautiful indoor pool to ease away your aches and pains, a comfortable lounge which can be hard to leave on a bad weather day and an excellent restaurant which can be hard to leave after a tasty fondue. And though it is no Albert Première, you can

38

stay here without blowing all of your
lottery winnings.

le montana***

☎ 0450 541499
📞 0450 540340
@ info@hotel-montana.fr
𝑊³ hotel-montana.fr
🛏 24 (b&b, ½)

In a quiet spot a little set back from the
main road into town, the Montana is just
200m from the Lognan cable car and is
equally close to the centre. Though it
lacks the cosy communal feel of the
Grands Montets hotel, the large chalet-
style building has spacious rooms, a
friendly welcome, a pleasant restaurant,
good facilities and private parking.

le dahu**

☎ 0450 540155
📞 -
@ -
𝑊³ -
🛏 22 (b&b, ½)

A pleasant and very well situated hotel,
right in the centre of town and less than
10 minutes walk from the cable car. The
Dahu is comfortable and inexpensive,
but perhaps the best thing about the
hotel is its restaurant, which serves very
good food and which has a terrace (open
to guests and public alike) that makes an
excellent spot for coffee drinking and
mountain watching.

les randonneurs*

☎ 0450 540280
📞 -
@ -
𝑊³ -
🛏 12 (b&b)

A very simple hotel providing beds
for cheap. Rooms range from a
dormitory to single or double
rooms either with basin or shower
(but no toilets). It's about as far away
from anything as it could be and still be
in Argentière, but if you want low-cost
digs then this is they.

39

accommodation

chalets

Chalet holidays cater for those who want to stay in a more relaxed setting, but don't want to fend for themselves. If you choose to stay in a chalet your options are either to book with a tour operator or to hunt out one that is privately run.

40

tour operators

Chamonix's popularity and proximity to Geneva makes it a prime location for tour operators, and accordingly almost every tour company in existence runs trips to the valley. There aren't any real chalets in the centre of town, but there are hundreds within a short walk and many more hundreds stretching the length of the valley. Some are basic and functional, some are plush and luxurious almost to the point of absurdity. The typical package is the same as anywhere else - bed, breakfast, afternoon tea and on all but 1 night of your stay an evening meal with wine. You will be looked after by at least one English chalet host. Tour companies will also organise flights and transfers, and some offer discounts for groups booking up an entire chalet. The rule of thumb is that the more you pay, the better you can expect the quality of everything to be. But unless you book the whole place you take pot-luck with your fellow guests - it can be a war zone or the beginning of a beautiful new friendship - but at least you know you all like snow.

independents

There are so many privately run chalets up and down the valley that to list them all would fill up half a book - no other resort has anything like the variety you'll find in the Chamonix valley.

Information on them is not as easy to find - the best place to start if you fancy this type of accommodation is the *Association des Propriétaires de Chalets* (t 0450 539230, i chamonixrentals.com or chamonix-chalets-appts.com), who keep a record of privately run chalets operating in the valley. Failing that, the Chamonix tourist office is a good bet, or the internet - some owners list their chalets on sites such as ifyouski.com or have their own websites. chamonet.com is also a good source. What is on offer in privately run chalets varies greatly. Some provide a similar package to those run by tour companies, some are bed & breakfast only, and in some you are left entirely to your own devices.

résidences

Résidences are effectively large and well appointed apartment blocks, such as you might find flanking the south side of the Thames in London. Most have their own gym, bar, swimming pool, sauna and so on - but they are basically self-catering accommodation with a nice foyer. The apartments house between 2 and 8 people, often in 2 or 3 adjoining rooms (some have up to 6) which will be kitted out with full kitchen facilities and bed linen - all you need to bring is some food.

The top end of the résidences market in Chamonix is Les Chalets du Savoy (4*, t 0450 535659, i les-chalets-du-savoy.com), a new construction on the north edge of town which pushes the limits of résidence luxury by offering fireplaces, satellite TV, catering and cleaning services. Not far behind is little brother Les Balcons du Savoy (4*, t 0450 503232, i les-balcons-du-savoy.com), perfectly located at the foot of Le Savoy beginners' slope and offering - amongst other things - covered parking and a babysitting service. Brand new down by the train station is La Ginabelle (4*, t 0450 553737, i residence-mgm.fr), an MGM project, and Cham Sud is home to Maeva La Riviere (3*, t 0450 532967) and a standard Pierre et Vacances offering (t 0450 534155).

Argentière's contribution to the résidences market is the glitzy-yet-friendly Crystal (4*, t 0450 502900, i lagrange-holidays.com) at the southern end of the strip, which has most of what you might be hoping for, though it is not as comprehensively furnished as the Savoy offerings in Chamonix.

At the extent of the valley the town of Montroc (just below Le Tour) is home to the Chalet Pierre Semard (2*, t 0450 540029, i chalet-hotel-psemard.com).

bed & breakfast

There are a handful of places that operate in the same way as your typical countryside b&b. More or less in Chamonix town are La Marjolaine (t 0450 530585), Les Arolles (t 0450 531430) and the Beauregard (t 0450 558 630), and heading a little further out are L'Oree du Bois (t 0450 555314) in Les Bossons and Les Marmottes (t 0450 533128) in Les Praz.

apartments

Ski apartments are typically compact and bijoux, and Chamonix does little to rock the tradition. There is luxury to be found, but most comprise 4 walls and a roof, within which you will generally find somewhere to sleep and somewhere to cook, and more often than not a tiny balcony on which to leave your skis or boards. Cham Sud is almost entirely made up of bog-standard apartments. As with private chalets there is an almost endless list of apartments available - to ease the process most are listed with rental agencies and if you shop around early enough you will more than likely be able to find something to suit. You can take your pick from any of the following: Agence des Drus (t 0450 533086, i agence-des-drus.com), Agence La Tour (t 0450 530853, i immobiliaire.la.tour.com), Agence Geralp (t 0450 534096), Agence la Montagne Grand Roc (t 0450 540879, i grand-roc.com), Agence Lamy Chamonix (t 0450 553300, i lamy-sa.fr), Peak Immobilier (t 0450 558414, i peak-immobilier.com), Agence Schuss (t 0450 540035, i chamonix-shuss.com), Agence

41

accommodation

Vacences (t 0450 540973) and France Location (t 0450 532841).

camping

Chamonix being a place for all comers, it is even equipped with a winter campsite, a few minutes south of Chamonix proper, in Les Bossons. It's not a field full of tents - but it is a field full of snow caravans, which isn't too different. The 'accommodation' is heated, has full washing facilities and even an on-site restaurant, but it's still a pretty basic experience. If this sounds like your thing, or you're very pressed for cash, Les Deux Glaciers (t 0450 531584) are the people to call.

a cheaper option

About 5 miles before you get to Chamonix, you pass a town that has developed a rather odd relationship with the rest of the valley. Its ski area is not part covered by the ChamSki pass, but it hosts Chamonix's slot in the World Cup downhill timetable. Few people who come to ski in Chamonix stay so far out - but a very large number of those who work in Chamonix live in Les Houches, including many ski instructors. The influx of foreign (and largely English) money into Chamonix's property market has raised the bar so high that for your average local it has become impossible to buy anything closer in. As a result Les Houches has become something of a haven for the French, and its dissociation with Chamonix skiing

means that it is very much a resort in its own right, with a character very much its own. If you would rather spend money on something other than accommodation, and go on a skiing holiday to escape the English, Les Houches might suit you better than Chamonix - if you don't mind an extra 15 minutes on your daily commute and prefer a small resort to a big town. The mountain is comparatively mild and almost entirely below the tree-line, so the slopes above Les Houches offer a very different kind of experience to skiing areas like Le Brévent or Les Grands Montets. Many of the pistes are red, but many of the reds are gentle in comparison to the rest of the valley. *La Verte*, the World Cup downhill run, is skiable in its entirety, and the pisted area is as big as Le Brévent or La Flégère. What there isn't is much off-piste, unless you're good in the trees - though if you are comfortable nipping in and out of the pines you'll have plenty to keep you happy and it is the best place in the valley to be in bad weather.

Most of Les Houches is suburban accommodation. There isn't really a centre - restaurants and bars (more of the restaurants) are dotted along the length of the road through the town. There's not much in the way of typical commerce either, aside from the obligatory ski rental shops. Though Chamonix is opening up to the dubious attractions of handbags that cost more than skis, Les Houches is not.

Information on hotels and standard accommodation is available from the tourist office. There are also a handful of privately owned and English-run chalets: 2 of the nicest are run by Chalet in the Mountains (t 0041 79242 8478, i chaletinthemountains.com). Les Houches also offers a couple of pleasant résidences as well - Les Grand Balcon (t 0479 650765, i eurogroup-vacences.com) and the MGM created Hauts de Chavants (2*, t 0450 546669, i residences-mgm.fr).

43

lift passes

Once you have arrived in Chamonix and found where you are staying, there are a few things to do before you can get on to the snow, of which buying a lift pass is one. Buying a lift pass in Chamonix can be a complicated business. Though you can simply buy a standard pass for the number of days you are in resort, because of the way the ski areas operate, the more money conscious skier can save the price of lunch by being careful about what - or when - to buy.

44

In 2003 Chamonix introduced a hands-free system. For passes that run over a number of days you now buy a card (€3) with an electronic chip that automatically opens the barriers at the entrance to the lifts. You can keep the card forever and simply recharge it when you want to ski. The system is being phased in for all the lifts in the valley - this is very much the fashion at the moment, with areas like Paradiski introducing the same system.

chamski or mont-blanc?

There are 2 main types of ski pass available in the Chamonix valley - the ChamSki pass and the Mont-Blanc pass. The ChamSki pass is the standard, and gives access to the 4 ski areas, the Aiguille du Midi cable car, the Montenvers railway and unlimited use of the Chamonix buses - pretty much everything you should want during your stay. The Mont-Blanc pass covers 10 resorts, and is something you are only likely to need if you are staying for a

snapshot

useful information
photo required for passes of 3 days or more
at peak times the queue for lift passes will be shorter at the Montenvers train station
if you lose your lift pass, it's lost
it can be cheaper to buy your lift pass on a daily basis
there are discounts for under 12s, under 16s, families and over 60s.

long time and have your own transport. The only potential drawback to the ChamSki pass is that it does not cover Les Houches. In addition , a pass for 4 days or more allows you 1 day's skiing in Courmayeur (through the Mont Blanc tunnel in Italy). A 6 day pass also comes with 2 free 'tickets-top', which you need to take the cable car from the Lognan mid-station to the top of Les Grands Montets (→ les grands montets). While the ChamSki pass may be the most convenient - and ChamSki sales account for over 95% of passes sold to English skiers - if you have a specific agenda to ski certain areas, or if you are an absolute beginner, it may be worth looking into other options. Morning, afternoon, and full-day passes for individual ski areas are available. If you are skiing 3 days and you ski 1 day in each of the 3 areas (for the single-day passes Le Brévent and La Flégère are considered one area) it works out cheaper to buy passes on a daily basis than to buy a 3 day ChamSki pass. This is because the ChamSki pass also gives access to the buses and to the Aiguille du Midi. In practice, if you are in ski gear you will never need to show a pass on the Chamonix bus - the significant difference is the Midi cable car, which is expensive without a ChamSki pass. But if you have no plans to ski the Vallée Blanche and are happy to miss out on the amazing view from the top of the Midi, buying single day passes may be the way to go.

handy to know

All the passes apart from season passes are available from any of the valley floor lift stations (including the Aiguille du Midi cable car), from the tourist office, and from the Montenvers train station. The Montenvers train station is also the only place where you can buy season passes. The tourist office is the easiest place to buy them - it has the longest opening hours and the most proficient English speaking staff. The kiosk at the Montenvers station is a good option at busy times, as it's less known about and therefore less crowded. It also has very different opening hours: 9am-5pm with no break for lunch, as opposed to 8:30am-12:30pm and 2:30pm-7:30pm.

The ChamSki pass is available for any number of days, and the longer the pass runs for the cheaper it is per day. The most common are the 3 and 6 day passes, for long weekends and week long holidays respectively. All sorts of deals are available, mostly aimed at **families** (➥ children), and it is worth reading the booklet on lift passes (available from the tourist office) or asking about offers when you buy your pass. If you are a complete *débutant* (**beginner**) and you expect to spend the majority of your time in the valley floor ski areas, you can buy a ChamStart pass, which will cover you just for those areas at a much lower price than the ChamSki. Extensions are available on a daily basis if you do decide to ski the main areas or if you want to meet friends on the mountain for lunch.

45

insurance (known as **carré neige**) is not included as standard with lift passes, but it is available for a small daily supplement - you will be asked whether or not you want it when you buy your pass. If you have not organised your own already, the insurance on offer is highly recommended. It covers you for all on-piste incidents, including blood wagon and helicopter recovery. If you are injured - and can produce a doctor's note - you can get a refund for the remains of a pass originally issued for 4 days or longer. Otherwise, the Compagnie du Mont-Blanc, who supply the passes and run the lifts, will not give you any kind of a refund for handing a pass back early. If you break your pass and can produce the remains, the tourist office will give you a replacement free of charge.

In spite of Chamonix being a town rather than a resort, it still feels as though every other shop is a ski rental shop (*location*). There are far too many shops to cover every one - what follows is an overview of ski and board rental and a brief description of some of the best places to go.

46

handy to know

All of the stores employ either competent or native **english** speakers, and all the staff know enough English to fit you with the right skis and boots... as with most places trying a little French won't hurt, but unless you are a confident speaker this is one area where it's probably best to operate in a language you are comfortable with.

Getting the **right equipment** will ensure you fully enjoy your holiday. Your feet will hurt if you don't get boots that fit well so don't be embarrassed to persevere until you find a pair that fits. If your boots cause you problems after you have tested them out, take them back - all the shops will help you find a more suitable pair. Unless you know you want a specific type or make of ski, take the advice of the ski fitter. They are the experts and will know which is the best ski for you based on your ability and age.

The majority of the rental places in Chamonix stock a decent range of **skis**. Rental prices do not vary much from shop to shop, so you may as well go to the one nearest to where you are staying - though some hotels and package holiday operators have deals with specific shops, usually for a 10% reduction on the rental price. If you want a specific brand of skis, you may have to hunt a little - most places carry Rossignol, Salomon and Dynastar but Atomics and some lesser known brands like Völkls are generally only found in the larger stores.

Renting a **board** is very different from renting skis. While most ski shops stock some boards and boots, they are generally old, poorly maintained and of no use to anyone except absolute beginners. If you want decent equipment, a specialist boarding shop is the place to go - also because the people serving you are likely to be boarders, so will have more of an idea what they are giving you. Chamonix has 4 boarding-specific shops.

At most shops you can take out **insurance** (except on test skis) to cover accidental breakage, loss or theft. Unfortunately skis do get stolen or taken by accident - with so many people skiing on similar skis it's easy to confuse yours with those belonging to somebody else. When you stop for lunch or après, it's a good idea to swap one of your skis with a friend so you both have a mis-matched pair. This helps ensure that nobody will pick up your skis, either by mistake or otherwise.

for skis

ravanel & co (valley c3) is a Salomon specialist based in Les Praz, in the car park by La Flégère lift. If you're staying in Chamonix it isn't worth heading out, as you can find Salomon skis in most rental places in town, but if you're in Les Praz this is probably the best of the small selection of rental shops. They also carry Salomon snowboards.

sanglard (e3) is a bit of a tardis - in spite of the small front, it is on 3 levels and carries an extensive range of outdoor clothing and equipment. Everything is well maintained and the staff know their stuff. There is also a branch in the Alpine Centre.

snell (d4) is possibly the largest outdoor store in Chamonix, and stocks a huge range of specialist clothing, footwear and equipment for almost any mountain pursuit. It also has a substantial rental section and employs enough staff to start a small army.

sport 2000 (e2) on Rue de la Gare just down from Chambre Neuf is a Rossignol specialist. The skis are very well maintained, the staff are friendly and professional people and the always-busy service shop out of the back of the store ensures all the skis are kept in excellent condition.

twinner (c4) is a big chain of stores with 2 in Cham Sud, 2 in the town centre and 1 in Argentière. They carry most brands of skis, and a wide range of outdoor clothing and accessories. They employ knowledgeable staff, and the equipment is well serviced and reliable.

ogier (e3) is one of a new chain of rental shops with a more customer friendly and modern approach than some places. It feels rather strange when you go in because the upstairs section sells coats and leather gloves and any number of things you don't need on a mountain. Downstairs is a sensible and good quality rental shop - and the biggest attraction of Ogier is that they stay open through lunch. It is also home to the Evolution 2 booking desk ($\rightarrow$ lessons & guiding).

for boards

invasion (f4) is just out of the north end of town, across the road from the hotel Alpina. Run by a Canadian, although it is relatively new it is probably the best in town for quality and personal service. They have a wide range of new boards to rent and will set up whatever bindings you want. They also stock Invasion and 686 clothing, and guitars, and there is a printing room in the store where you can get your own designs put onto a t-shirt or car sticker.

otavalo (f4) on the north edge of town is a specialist boarding and telemarking shop. All the boards have Flow bindings and they are all well serviced and in decent condition. Otavalo is French run and it's a good idea to have a go with whatever French you have.

trajectoire (c4) is another Flow specialist, small and very well run with a good selection of boards to rent or buy. The staff speak excellent English and are both friendly and very enthusiastic about their chosen sport.

48

zero-g (c4) has a sales shop and a rental place that also sells last season's equipment at discount prices. French-run, all staff are riders themselves, and while the rental place feels a bit like a Poundsaver, the equipment and service are good.

for other equipment

Rental shops offer a lot more than just skis and boards. You can hire touring skis, telemarks, snowblades, avalanche transceivers, snowshoes... in fact more or less anything you might conceivably need or want for the outdoors. The more specialist your requirement, the more likely you are to have to go to a large store - like Twinner, Snell or Sanglard - to find it.

ski schools

Chamonix is the centre of the ESF (*Ecole de Ski Français*), and on the slopes red-jacketed Frenchmen abound - especially during school holidays, when there are up to 300 *moniteurs* (instructors) in resort. With such a dominant presence there are a number of advantages to learning with the ESF. If you look closely, however, there are other ski schools too. Many are primarily guiding companies, but this doesn't mean they don't do ski lessons, and for native English instruction or less of a production-line feel you would be well served to shop around a bit.

Chamonix is a challenging place to ski no matter what your level of ability, and there is instruction to suit all. You will not so much see trains of youngsters zig-zagging down the slopes as you will see groups of boarders perfecting 360s and skiers working their turns on the slalom course. Even experts will find new things to try - though for that you are better off employing a guide.

specifics

prices are pretty standard across the board for all disciplines - though you may pay a little more for the smaller companies there's not much in it. If you book group lessons with the ESF or Evo 2, you can have a week's worth of half-day instruction for only a little more than it costs to rent your skis. Private lessons (and guides) are a different story, but you won't find too much

variation in what the different schools charge.

group lessons are the cheapest way to learn to ski. When you book you will be asked your level of skiing/boarding ability, either by the vague 'beginner/intermediate/advanced' pigeonholes, by the colour of piste you are comfortable on or the number of weeks you have skied before. In practice the divisions aren't as accurate as they could be - some people overestimate their ability or misunderstand words like 'confident' and 'controlled', so to an extent the level of your group is pot luck. If you are honest about your skill level you are likely to find yourself (vaguely) in the right place.

If you have the money, **private lessons** are without question the way forward. Once you're past the basics, individual attention is the best way to significantly improve your technique and is often better value. If you can get a group of four or more the individual price per day is similar to the average price per day for group lessons, with the advantage that you go where you want to go and practise what you want to practise. The length of private lessons varies from school to school, but generally the divisions are simply for a half day (morning or afternoon) or a full day. A half day will be 3 hours of instruction on one side of lunch. Generally, if you book private lessons

49

your instructor(s) will have their own transport and so will be able to pick you up from wherever you are - very useful in the Chamonix valley.

Not all of the small companies offer **snowboard** lessons, so check before you try to book. The skill divisions, prices, times and overall format is much the same as with skiing.

50

Either make your **booking** before you get to Chamonix - by email, fax or phone - or once you're in resort, in person at the ski school office. Always pre-book in peak season, as there are not enough instructors to meet demand - schools recommend booking at least 2 weeks in advance. To confirm your booking, the schools will need your name, level of ability and a credit card number.

The schools have different **meeting points**. The ESF group lessons congregate en masse either outside the Maison de la Montagne (e4) or by the Cham Sud main bus stop (a3/4). Evo 2 will tell you where to meet when you book, and the smaller companies will generally be pretty flexible as the majority of their lessons are private engagements.

It is illegal to teach in France without a qualification recognised by the French establishment. In effect this means that the majority of **instructors** in France are French, as few other 'international'

qualifications are accepted and the equivalence race test that foreign instructors must pass is extremely difficult. But this approach gives you the advantage of knowing that your instructor is at the least a very competent skier or boarder.

Almost all instructors speak good **english** and there are also instructors who speak every other language - though you will need to book a long way in advance should you want instruction in a language less common to the Alps.

Lessons take place **whatever the weather**, unless the entire lift system is closed in which case the school will refund the full lesson price. They will also refund you if you are ill or have an accident and can produce a valid medical certificate. If you cancel a lesson for any other reason, your chances of getting a refund are relative to how much notice you give the school, and how charming you are when you cancel.

esf

☎ 0450 532257
📞 0450 536530
@ infoski@esf-chamonix.com
W³ esf.net/chamonix   _April 2006_
🖥 place de l'eglise

The French leviathan exerts a stronger hold over the market here than perhaps any other resort - the Chamonix branch is the headquarters of the whole ESF operation. It is the oldest ski school in the Alps, and becoming an instructor is a difficult enough process that you are guaranteed a quality skier as your teacher. What you are not guaranteed is that you will be taught the latest techniques - older instructors who themselves learned on older skis may not be entirely up to speed on carving. It has been said that there are as many ways to ski as there are ESF instructors. On the other side of the coin, many of the younger instructors teach both skiing and snowboarding, and there are charismatic and competent teachers in abundance - and all are advertised as being proficient English speakers. Lessons in all types of discipline are available, including "new school" and cross-country, and lessons for disabled skiers, and all run throughout the whole season - not just during the school holidays as at some of the smaller schools. Argentière has its own ESF office (t 0450 540012, i esf-argentiere-valleedechamonix.com).

evolution 2

☎ 0820 821024
📞 0450 559133
@ chamonix@evolution2.com
W³ evolution2.com
🖥 ogier (rue joseph vallot)

51

A younger, smaller, and fresher alternative to the ESF, Evolution 2 is one the best respected and fastest growing ski schools in the Alps. Their innovative approach is more overtly about being a little wacky, and there's none of the fusty mustiness of the ESF hierarchy. Alongside general skiing and snowboarding Evo 2 offer courses for women-only, weekends, technical off-piste skills as well as heliskiing... away from skis you can use them for paragliding, winter mountaineering, showshoeing, dog sledding, and also helicopter and hot-air balloon flights. If you can think it up, they probably cover it.

all mountain performance

☎ 0450 532833
📞 0450 558399
@ info@allmountainperformance.com
W³ allmountainperformance.com
🖥 -

A new specialist school, AMP offers private ski instruction for all levels alongside a programme of courses and clinics for advanced skiers. Run by an Englishman with close ties to Evo 2, some of the courses are run by Evo 2 instructors - but the emphasis here is very much on the top level of skiing, all over the mountain, in any conditions. The school is well connected in Chamonix's English community, and you can also book accommodation (through High Mountain Holidays) and transfers (through ATS). The boss is a BASI trainer, and AMP also offers instructor training for anyone with their sights on the international licence. Bookings for any of the courses can be made through the English office (t 01279 830308).

52

mcnab mountain sports

☎ 0450 542284
📞 -
@ info@mcnab.co.uk
W³ mcnab.co.uk
🖃 scotland/argentière

No one called Andy, no guns and no parachuting behind enemy lines - McNab is a family run snowboard specialist, offering all-in packages of chalet accommodation, lift pass and instruction or guiding (they also organise transfers, but this is not included in the price). It is a small set-up, and the courses they run depend on what week it is - sometimes it's beginner's stuff, other weeks it's backcountry exploration - roughly aligned to coincide with what the weather and snow conditions ought to be like. They have a Scottish base, and you can book on the Scotland number (01546 830243).

summit

☎ 0450 540511
📞 0450 540081
@ info@aventureentete.com
W³ aventureentete.com
🖃 620 route du plagnolet, argentière

The smallest of the companies offering group lessons, Summits is a team of ESI qualified French guides. Their service is excellent and if their English is sometimes a little questionable, their passion for Chamonix is not. They only offer a limited selection of non-skiing activities, and their main attraction is that with their weekly group trip down the Vallée Blanche you can get yourself a run down the glacier on the cheap.

ski sensations

☎ 0450 535646
📞 0450 535646
@ info@ski-sensations.com
W³ ski-sensations.com
🖃 31 allée du savoy

A small and very enthusiastic team who offer group lessons called "mini-technical" courses along with off-piste trips, mountain awareness courses, ice climbing, and paragliding. Their office hours are frustratingly short (since they spend most of their time on the slopes), so enquiries and bookings are best made over the phone, and a long time beforehand if you are planning an trip during high season.

guides

To experience everything Chamonix has to offer, you will need to hire a guide. The glaciated terrain away from the valley's pisted areas is life-threatening to the inexperienced - but a guide can make possible to the intermediate skier what even an expert would hesitate to try unaided.

The difference between **guides** and ski **instructors** is fundamental. Instructing is about 'how', and guiding is about 'where'. Ski instructors are not qualified to take you off-piste, and you should not ask them to. In contrast, the limiting factor with a mountain guide is your own ability. If you are competent enough they will take you anywhere you want to go.

There is no question of a guide's **ability**. Becoming a guide takes years, and requires an intimate knowledge of everything the mountains have to offer. While they are invariably expert skiers, first and foremost they are mountaineers: they have extensive experience of the procedure and practice of mountain rescue, are proficient rock and ice climbers, are competent and comfortable in all types of conditions... they are the very definition of a safe pair of hands.

In addition to their skills on the mountain, guides will provide you with all the extra **equipment** needed on a trip: avalanche transceivers, harnesses,

ropes, ice axes, crampons... all this is included in the initial price. Also, for Vallée Blanche trips your guide will reserve a place on the cable car, leaving you with more time to get worried about the hike down the arête. As with private lessons, the downside to hiring a guide is the price. A full day can cost up to €300 - but you are better off spending the money and coming back alive.

53

And what's on offer? Anything you can think of. Along with the Vallée Blanche, you can hire a guide to travel the Chamonix-Zermatt haute route, ski the Pas de Chevre, or simply to take you to where the powder is. Some companies offer mountain safety courses, ski-touring courses, rock- and ice-climbing trips, snowshoe expeditions... the list is as long as the mountains are high. Along with private bookings, most companies run a regular group trip down the Vallée Blanche. They will also show you around the pistes - but don't expect them to be too excited about doing it. Prices vary depending upon the activity - as an approximate rule of thumb you should expect to pay around €300 for a full day with a guide (and guides can only be booked on a full day basis), sometimes a little less if you're just skiing the Vallée Blanche.

There are more guides working in Chamonix than in any other resort in the Alps, and as a result there are a number of choices when reserving a guide. Most guides are very impressive, so whoever you book with you are unlikely to be let down. Along with in-depth local knowledge, guides have an ingrown passion for the mountains and a very professional approach to their vocation. The members of the Chamonix Bureau des Guides are taken solely from the town's indigenous population (known as Chamoniards). Those guides who work for the Bureau are both aware and proud of its traditions, and you can be sure that whoever your guide, you will receive top class service - though the jacket might spoil your colour-coordinated photos. In additions, because there is such a demand for guides, some companies have been established in the valley to provide this service and focus only on off-piste skills and ski mountaineering.

There is a sizeable community of guides who work largely without attachment to a particular company or the Bureau. They are more authentic mountain men than career guides, and most spend as much time doing their own climbing and mountaineering as they do working. Most of their business comes through word-of-mouth, and because they are not constrained by company guidelines they are the best place to go for unusual requests like ice-climbing by head-torch, or for a moonlight descent of the Vallée Blanche.

chamonix experience

☏ 0450 540936
📞 0450 540988
@ info@chamex.com
W³ chamex.com
🖅 the alp centre (argentière)

A more far-reaching company than most - in addition to the regular excursions they offer a range of specialist courses and a programme of extended trips across the Alps and throughout the world year-round. Many of the team are native English speakers, and the Argentière-based company is fronted by Russell Brice, whose prowess on the mountain is matched only by his renown in the bar. Cham Ex employ a number of Chamonix's independent guides on a freelance basis, and are well placed to find somebody on short notice. This is also the place to go if you want to work out a way to do something unusual - and their office is also the only proper coffee shop in Argentière (➥ argentière).

stages et expéditions

☏ 0450 559426
📞 0450 558399
@ info@stages-expeditions.com
W³ stages-expeditions.com
🖅 chemin des seyllires, les bossons

Based out in Les Bossons, S&E is kind of the French equivalent of Cham Ex, in that it has a well-known front-man and is more interested in mountains than in skiing the tamed stuff. If you like the idea of touring, climbing Mont Blanc, and pottering around the mountains of the world in the company of Frenchmen, S&E are your perfect match.

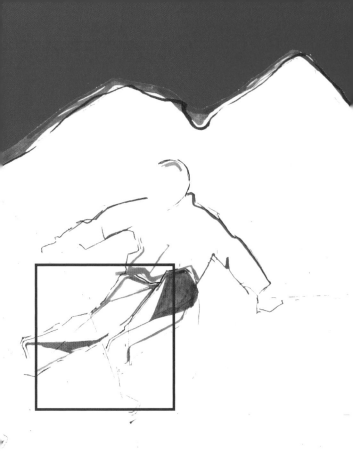

the skiing

Chamonix is a place to test your limits, and to extend them. The mountains offer a multitude of challenges to skier and boarder alike, but there are few enough easy runs that the faint-hearted will more than likely find themselves skiing the same stretch over and over. If you are willing, Chamonix will drag you out of your comfort zone - but if you are looking to cruise around within your envelope, you will probably be disappointed.

58

pistes

Considering Chamonix's enormous popularity, the number of pistes in the valley is surprisingly small. The total length of groomed runs is only 150kms, so unlike huge areas such as the 3 Vallées or the Espace Killy, the Chamonix ski areas do not make for long day trips - if that is what you want, you will have to hire a guide and head off piste.

The piste system follows the same colour-coding used in all ski areas throughout Europe (→ 'pistes' in the glossary). Chamonix, though, has a higher than average proportion of steep runs. The blues are a little redder than in most resorts, and the reds a little blacker... the company on-piste is generally a little more aggressive too. In addition to this, you should only use the piste colour-coding as a general guide. Although the gradient or width of each individual piste stays the same, other features such as snow conditions can

snapshot

vital statistics
150kms of pistes - 7 greens, 20 blues, 17 reds & 9 blacks
36 lifts - 6 cable cars, 3 gondolas, 17 chairs & 10 drags
off-piste - the vallée blanche & vast backcountry
highest point - 3842m
longest run - approx 22kms

change daily. A blue piste can become more testing than a nearby red, because it is over-crowded with skiers of ranging abilities or because of poor or icy conditions. And personal feelings about pistes vary greatly - an easy blue to one skier can seem like a vertical drop to another.

off-piste

The opportunities for off-piste skiing in the valley are almost unlimited. Apart from at Le Tour there are few marked itineraries, but there are a number of black runs which are unpisted and comparable to anything you might find above Verbier in Switzerland's 4 Vallées. But Chamonix's real off-piste is out of sight of any lift. Alongside and in between pistes in most areas you will find plenty of ungroomed snow on which to practise your off-piste technique without having to venture too far.

lifts

As with the pistes, the lifts are not about comfort. The resort is guaranteed popularity because of the excellent skiing, and for a long time the need to update the lifts was ignored. Recently the Compagnie du Mont-Blanc has begun a programme of refits - the liaison cable car between Le Brévent and La Flégère has made a huge difference to skiing from Chamonix town, and the Bochard bubble on Les Grands Montets is an efficient and welcome addition to the options from Lognan. There are plans to put in a lift to connect the small town of Vallorcine (out of the valley over the Col de Montets) to the Tête de Balme chair on the backside of Le Tour, and to drag the valley's older and less comfortable lifts into the 21st century... but it will be a gradual process, and for the time being there remains a mix of old and new.

Most of the lifts open from early December - the remainder being operational by about Christmas. Le Brévent and La Flégère are the first to close, around the middle of April, and Le Tour follows shortly afterwards. The lifts on Les Grands Montets often run into early May, though the exact dates change yearly and if the snow conditions are good, the lifts may open earlier or close later than advertised. During shorter daylight hours in the depths of winter, the lifts close earlier in the day than later in the season when there is light for longer. Opening and closing times are noted at the bottom of some lifts, or alternatively the tourist office will have full details of

approximate times for the whole season.

the areas

Chamonix has 4 ski areas, each of which are described separately in this section, in the following order:
le brévent (map a)
la flégère (map b)
les grands montets (map c)
le tour (map d)
In this chapter you'll find a description of how to get to and from the slopes, the general characteristics and aspect of the area, and detail of the pistes, the off-piste, the mountain restaurants and the local après for each area. At the back of the book there is a more detailed table of lift information and a ski map for each area (in which the piste colours correspond to those used by the resort).

59

Avril 2001

beginners

Thousands of people of all ages choose to learn in Chamonix. In many ways it is the ideal place for beginners, in spite of perceived difficulties and the widely held belief that learning in Chamonix is a bad idea. It is true that there are few gentle slopes in the valley, and other resorts are more generous with free lifts for beginners. And because of the detached ski areas a lunchtime rendezvous between learners and non-learners needs prior planning. But it is perfectly possible to learn here, and thanks to the ChamStart pass it can be far cheaper for absolute beginners to learn in Chamonix than anywhere else.

If you have never worn plastic boots or strapped yourself to a plank of wood, the valley has 4 learners' areas. They can get very busy, but being away from the main ski areas you are not constantly worrying about faster skiers shooting past and knocking you over - and the lift pass is much cheaper.

le savoy is a very gentle slope that isn't very wide so when busy it's like trying to ski to the toilets in a crowded pub. It is, however, an excellent location for children, as it's right in the middle of town. The top of the slope is next to the Brévent gondola, so people use the drag lift to avoid walking up the hill in the mornings - at 9am it can be amazingly busy. There is a small buvette that sells snacks and drinks.

On the other side of town to Le Savoy, **les planards** is for those who are a step up the ability ladder. It offers an introduction to chairlifts, a gentle blue through the trees and a straight but rather narrow red. It is also the end of the run down from the Vallée Blanche, so from midday onwards you'll see parties with harnesses and big smiles skiing down or eating in the Luge d'Eté restaurant. It tends to be less busy in the morning than other valley floor slopes, but for a reason - until the sun gets there around midday, it can be very cold.

Two gentle runs a short walk away from Les Grands Montets cable car, **les chosalets** is to Argentière what Le Savoy is to Chamonix - a good spot for children and absolute beginners.

Higher up the valley alongside the Le Tour gondola, **la vormaine** has snow earlier - and later - than slopes lower down. It gets busy, but it is a large and very open space, with either 2 or 3 runs depending on how it's pisted. Often 1 run is left ungroomed as a powder practice area. As there is little difference between its runs and the gentle blues higher up the mountain at Le Tour, so when you feel you're ready to progress you need only walk to the gondola station and head on up.

intermediates

If you are looking to push yourself to the next level, Chamonix is the ideal place to

60

do it. Le Brévent and La Flégère have a variety of red runs and all of Les Grands Montets is challenging: unless you spend all your time at Le Tour, you are likely to have to work pretty hard on many of the runs. If you want to improve your technique on moguls, Les Grands Montets has a limitless choice, some of which is relatively gentle. For powder practice, Le Brévent and La Flégère have good variety but Le Tour has the most open space that isn't too steep.

experts

You will not want for adventure. The pistes will test you and dare you to go faster, and the off-piste will amaze you, scare you, and remind you who's in charge. All 4 ski areas have something for the expert, and away from the pistes there is no limit as to what is on offer - the only downside is that to fully appreciate the valley you need to hire a guide, partly because a wrong turn can put you in a lot of danger and partly because unless you really know the area, without one you are unlikely to find the best of what there is.

boarders

Chamonix is superb for all aspects of boarding. The steep slopes make a great place to learn or to hone your technique, and there are abundant hits and lips in the natural terrain. All but 2 or 3 of the runs can be accessed without taking a draglift. Though Les Grands Montets snowpark is largely ignored, freestylers can get their fix

down in Les Bossons - in every way it is difficult to think of a better destination to push you to the limits of your ability and beyond.

non-skiers

The main attraction for non-skiers is the Aiguille du Midi, standing at 3842m. On a clear day it commands extraordinary views of the valley and the Alps beyond, along with the more immediate spectacle of skiers hiking down the arête that is the start of the Vallée Blanche. From the viewing platforms you may also see extreme skiers heading down in various other directions, or mountaineers and climbers heading up the surrounding slopes and peaks. The construction itself is incredible, and the cable car ride alone will get your pulse racing... and the air is thin enough at the top to make you short of breath just from walking up stairs. Temperatures on the Aiguille can be as low as -30°C, though the sun can feel hot on a sunny day in late season - the best approach is to take a number of layers.

For those unwilling to brave the Midi cable car the view from the top of Le Brévent is an impressive - though utterly incomparable - alternative. As far as mountain walks go, though there are endless trails in the valley there is little for non-skiers in the 4 pisted areas.

61

le brévent

The only ski area directly accessible from Chamonix town, Le Brévent has something for everyone: gentle pistes for beginners and intermediates to practise on; fast and challenging reds and blacks for the more advanced; narrow couloirs and wide powder bowls for those in search of untracked powder. It also boasts awe inspiring views of Mont Blanc and the Aiguille du Midi, and with the cable car link to La Flégère the combined pisted area is the largest in the valley.

62

Stretching above Chamonix on the north side of the valley, the slopes of Le Brévent face predominantly south and south-east. By mid-afternoon Le Brévent peak obscures the sun on some pistes (notably the Charles Bozon - the black from the top of the Brévent cable car), but the majority of the area catches a few rays for most of the day.

getting there

The gondola station is a short walk from the centre of town - but it's a short very steep walk, so the best way to get there is to head to Le Savoy nursery slope and take the draglift, which takes you to just above the base of the gondola. If you are driving there, you can park your car in the multi-storey just above the gondola for a small hourly charge - it has spaces even in peak season.

Le Brévent has the most efficient base station, and queues rarely last long. At 9am the line moves more slowly

map a

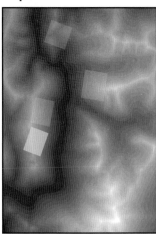

snapshot

out of interest
highest point - 2500m
aspect - s & se
access - gondola, cable car liaison with la flégère
lifts - 1 cable car, 5 chairs & 2 drags
pistes - 1 green, 5 blue, 3 red & 2 blacks
off-piste - couloirs, bowls
restaurants - 3

highlights & hotspots
the panorama from le panoramic
the charles bozon black
the only area accessible from the town
long lift queues at the end of the day

the Source and the Charlanon lifts, the blue track leading back to the Cornu chairlift is narrow but rarely busy, so it's not a bad place to practise away from the traffic.

For anyone of intermediate level or above a major highlight is the Cornu chair, which leads to 2 excellent **red** runs - a wide and sweeping piste back down to the bottom of the lift and a sustained slope off the back that leads towards the Flégère liaison. Conditions are consistently good throughout most of the day and both are varied enough to be skied again and again. For those graduating from blues, the 2 reds down the Charlanon chair are almost always quiet, and have short steep sections that are ideal for getting in a few turns without getting out of control.

because the ESF classes take priority, and when the resort is busy - or when the Flégère cable car is closed due to high wind - expect to wait up to a half hour.

pistes

There is 1 short **green** run from the top of the Parsa chair, also accessible from the Altitude 2000 chairlift. It has its own easy draglift, and there is almost no high speed traffic so it is an unthreatening - and sunny - place to learn.

With the exception of the initial green stretch that runs under the lift, all of the runs down from the Parsa chair are **blues** of varying gradients. They are only loosely marked as pistes - you can pretty much choose where you go and the area is large enough to keep you entertained for quite a while - with a few natural rollers and lips for the more adventurous. Elsewhere, from the top of

The Charles Bozon **black** run from the top of the cable car is the best known of all the pistes on Le Brévent. Though quite short it is very fast, and in the middle section you have the option of skiing one of the steepest mogul fields in the valley. The snow surface tends to be icy in the early morning, and by mid-afternoon there will be flat light on the top section as the sun is obscured by the Brévent peak. There can also be lengthy queues for the cable car - the best times to go are late morning or over lunch when everyone else is tucking in to steak and chips. The only other black is accessed from the back of

63

the Cornu chair - as the red piste bends right and becomes a track, straight down is a short, steep run that tends to be mogulled by the afternoon, and towards the end of the season will be slushy by lunchtime.

off-piste

There is extensive off-piste from the top of the Brévent cable car - as long as you know where you're going. Under the Cornu chair are 2 narrow couloirs that make for good practise with easy access. For an introduction to powder, a bumpy traverse to the right of the main Cornu piste followed by a short climb leads you to a wide bowl where the fresh snow doesn't get tracked out as fast as most places. It is also possible to make your way over to La Flégère without taking the liaison cable car, by climbing up from the top of the Cornu, then by way of the Col de la Glière down to the Combe Lachenal - but depending on the snow cover this will involve some hiking, skinning or snowshoeing, and the drop-in to the Combe de la Glière is a 35°-40° slope.

eating & drinking

The **altitude 2000** restaurant (t 0450 531558) is reached by the Alt 2000 or La Parsa chairlifts. A large and very busy restaurant, it has a decent menu of snacks, pizzas, full-blown meals and overgrown desserts. Service is not high-speed, but the food when it arrives will be more than enough to satisfy the

64

appetite you work up while you wait. It's a little more expensive than Le Brévent's other 2 restaurants, presumably because it is slightly more accessible and has a large outdoor section with a wind-break.

la bergerie (t 0450 530542) at the top of the gondola is probably the best Le Brévent has to offer. There is a table-service restaurant upstairs and a self-service counter on the lower floor. There are terraces on both levels. The restaurant is fine, service is efficient and friendly and the self-service section is the only place on Le Brévent where you don't have to wait around for someone to bring you your food - and the huge tartiflette pan is enough to make anyone's mouth water. The only let down is the hot drinks, which are served in tiny polystyrene cups that barely hold enough to satisfy a small mouse.

At the top of the cable car, **le panoramic** (t 0450 534411) is the place to go for great views. The higher you go the bigger Mont Blanc seems, and on a clear day the panorama out of the valley is fabulous (hence the name). The table service is generally slow, but the scenery makes the waiting much more bearable. You can take the cable car down again if you don't fancy the black run on a full stomach.

None of the restaurants on Le Brévent have **picnic** rooms. Probably the best places to pull out your thermos and unwrap your sandwiches are at the top of the Cornu chair and the top of the Brévent cable car (at the launching point for the Charles Bozon black run) - though the latter can get very busy with tourists.

From the gondola station it is only a 5 minute walk to the centre of town, but if you need a drink before heading down the hill - or if you are waiting to meet someone - a small bar just along the road provides the perfect spot for après. **la cabolée** becomes a restaurant in the evening, but from lunchtime onwards it is open for the usual après mix of vin chaud, beer, and a deliciously sweet hot chocolate. Head to the main road below the lift station, turn right, and it is 30 yards away, opposite the Savoyarde hotel.

bad weather

There aren't many options on Le Brévent when the weather closes in. If it's snowing heavily, the chances are the whole area will be shut, and as the weather clears it will re-open gradually, with the Brévent cable car being the last thing to get going again. Often after a dump of fresh snow La Bergerie restaurant becomes very full of people waiting to catch the first cable car up... but if it's snowing you are probably better off heading elsewhere.

getting home

When the resort is busy, even getting

back to the gondola station to get back down to the town can be a process - the 4-man chair at La Parsa doesn't deal well with the traffic, and you may find yourself doing a lot of standing around. The queue for the gondola down will start to grow at about 3:30 in the afternoon. By 4pm there will probably be about a half-hour line - if you want to avoid queuing, head down at around 3pm or ski down (if the run is open). The Nants run leads back to town from the bottom of the Parsa chair - and is an excellent way to avoid the afternoon queue for the gondola. It is marked on the map as a piste, but is groomed only once or twice a year, and is often closed due either to avalanche danger or rockfall. It is rated black thanks to a very steep top section, which becomes ledgy and nasty if there hasn't been snow for a while. After that, a winding track through the trees leads down to the gondola and the top of Le Savoy nursery slope - allowing you to ski all the way into town if you want to.

65

la flégère

There are only 5 lifts on the Flégère, but the total skiable area is surprisingly large and aside from a gentle lower section the runs are steep and challenging. It is a bit like a mini version of Les Grands Montets, and is home to the Index, a wide and exposed mountain face accessed by the Darth Vader lift. You'll understand the name when you see it.

As with Le Brévent, the majority of slopes face south and south-east - which is good for sun, but resulting in slushy spring snow in late season. Many of Le Flégère's runs are quite exposed and conditions can be very cold when the wind is up.

getting there

La Flégère is within walking distance if you're staying in Les Praz, otherwise it's a bus journey. If you drive there be careful as you enter the car park: the odd one way system takes you in on the left hand side, though a lot of people don't see the signs - or choose to ignore them. You have to cross back to the right hand side as you leave... the best advice is to be cautious. The car park is not as large as it seems and it fills up fast, so get there early.

In contrast with the efficiency of Le Brévent, La Flégère's cable car system is slow, and worse it is often closed because of high winds - sometimes even when there's no noticeable wind on the valley floor. Queues can look

map b

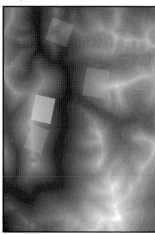

66

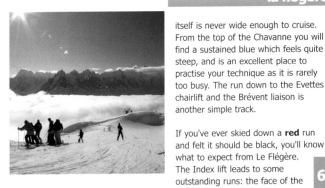

deceptively short because they continue inside the cable car building, so if you can see a queue outside then you probably have a half hour wait. When it's busy it is just as fast to go to Le Brévent and take the liaison cable car across - and this is the thing to do when the Flégère cable car is closed, as the skiing will probably still be open and you may find you have all the pistes to yourself.

pistes

There are 2 **green** runs, both down to the right as you come out of the cable car. They are fed by a narrow track, which makes for bust-ups between beginners and faster skiers heading for the Chavanne lift.

The **blue** run from the Index is basically just a track, and can be difficult to follow. It is useful as an access piste if you are looking for bumps or fresh powder, but the run

itself is never wide enough to cruise. From the top of the Chavanne you will find a sustained blue which feels quite steep, and is an excellent place to practise your technique as it is rarely too busy. The run down to the Evettes chairlift and the Brévent liaison is another simple track.

If you've ever skied down a **red** run and felt it should be black, you'll know what to expect from Le Flégère. The Index lift leads to some outstanding runs: the face of the Index mountain, back down underneath the lift, is as steep a red as you are likely to find. The highlight of the Index's options is perhaps the Combe Lachenal, the start of which is a short walk from the top of the lift. It is long, steep, wide, and sustained, and takes you all the way down to the Brévent liaison and the Evettes chair. From the Floria drag behind the Index lift, you reach a very long red that runs all the way down to La Trappe.

Though some of the reds blur the boundary, only 1 run is rated **black** - the initial section to the right as you head down from the Floria drag. It is a short and steep descent that then becomes a red for the lower section down to La Trappe.

off-piste

You don't have to hunt for powder on La Flégère - so much of the area is wide open and unpisted. There are plenty of options down from the Floria drag towards La Trappe, and if you want tree skiing then take the Evettes chair and head straight back down under the lift. La Flégère is also the launching point for a number of single day touring routes to Le Buet, just out of the head of the valley on the other side of the Col des Montets (➥ off-piste & touring).

eating & drinking

Le Flégère doesn't have much to offer for lunch - in the cable car station there is a standard fare restaurant and bar, and just outside by the Index lift is a snack stop which plays a distracting mix of less-than-mainstream music. Away from the cable car there is only one option.

Designed as a sun-trap, **la chavanne** (t 0450 530613) is basically just a snack bar, serving hot and cold sandwiches and baguettes. It is, however, well placed to catch the weather, and you'll need to be early or lucky to get a lounger on the sundeck.

There are plenty of perfect **picnic** spots by the side of the green runs down to La Trappe - or if you want spectacular views then you can't do better than the top of the Index, where you have a panorama starting from the 4122m Verte peak and the Drus above Argentière, across the jagged Aiguille de Chamonix range that leads to the Aiguille du Midi and Mont Blanc.

Like Le Brévent, you'll have to head down for après and even then Les Praz does not have a busy **après** scene. But if you want food or a relaxing drink you have a number of choices. The Eden hotel (➥ hotels) has a bar and family room, which are open all day. The Lanchers hotel has a cosy bar, and the Cabine restaurant by the golf course serves excellent food if you have more time to spare.

bad weather

While the cable car often closes in strong winds, when there is low visibility the Evettes chairlift is one of the few in the valley that remains open, and will be one of the first to re-open after a heavy fall - if the cable car is closed you can reach the chairlift by taking the liaison from Le Brévent. The piste the chairlift serves is a track, but straight back down under the lift is a wooded area, which offers a short but sweet (and steep) combat ski.

getting home

The run back down to Les Praz is a pleasant ski home - a track through the trees with a more open area towards the bottom. In contrast to the runs higher up the mountain, it is rated black when it barely feels like a red. If it is open, it is by far the best way to get back down to town as the inefficiency of the cable car means that there are often queues to get back down to Les Praz. They can be considerable in high season - and as with the journey up the mountain in the morning much of the queue is inside the building so don't be fooled just because you can't see a line. In windy conditions the cable car is often closed, so you may find that you have to take the liaison cable car over to Le Brévent and come down into Chamonix town - though if this is the case the Chamonix bus runs a special shuttle service back to the car park in Les Praz.

69

les grands montets

There is nothing forgiving about Les Grands Montets. If skiing is about steep stuff, fast stuff, bumps, and wide open ungroomed space, this is one of the best areas in the Alps, and probably the world. The runs are demanding even for the most able skier, and after a week without snowfall the entire mountain face looks like a mogul field. Even the beginners' slope is relatively steep. Along with the Vallée Blanche, Les Grands Montets is why people come to the Chamonix valley.

The slopes of Les Grands Montets face mostly north and north-west, and as a result have by far the best snow conditions in the valley. It is the first area to open at the start of the season, and the last to close - with lifts usually running well into May. It gets no sunshine before about 11am, and in the height of winter can be very cold indeed, especially at 3233m at the top of the Grands Montets cable car.

getting there

There is a pedestrian route to the cable car from the centre of Argentière - if you're any further afield your only option is the bus.

If you intend to drive the free car park is very large and not too well organised. If it's busy there will be security directing you to a space - but if it's busy you are best off parking close to the exit: come 5 o'clock there can be an enormous jam as hundreds of people

map c

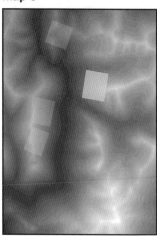

snapshot

out of interest
highest point - 3233m
aspect - n & nw
access - cable car & chairlift
lifts - 1 cable car, 5 chairs & 1 gondola
pistes - 1 green, 4 blue, 2 red & 3 black
off-piste - endless: wide, exposed, moguls, trees, glaciated
restaurants - 5

highlights & hotspots
queues and more queues
possibly the best bumps in the alps
the plan joran restaurant

pistes

While the beginners' slope that runs alongside the terrain park may technically be a **green** run, it is as steep as many a blue. Worse, it serves as the run-off for a number of other pistes, meaning it is in constant use by high-speed traffic heading back to Lognan. Not a place for the faint-hearted learner.

There's not much true **blue** on Les Grands Montets: the runs that are rated blue serve mainly as access to powder and bump runs. Don't go looking for long cruisey pistes, because you won't find them.

As an improving intermediate you have a variety of **red** choices: short and simple run from Les Marmottes; long and winding from the Bochard bubble; the narrow run that feeds the mogul fields under the Herse chairlift... there is no shortage of steep space to ski.

The marking of **blacks** on Les Grands Montets is a little misleading. The Chamois run from the Bochard bubble is intended as a mogul run, and the winding track is there only as a dropping-off point. More importantly, the famous runs from the top of the Grands Montets cable car (the Point de Vue and Les Pylons) are never groomed, so while they are marked and patrolled as pistes, the conditions are very variable. With fresh snow, the run back to Lognan will be pure powder -

try to leave at the same time, but if you are parked at the main-road end of the car park you will be able to saunter past all the frustrated drivers and head straight back to town. Alternatively you could park your car in Argentière.

You have 2 choices to get to the skiing. The cable car to the Lognan mid-station is the obvious route, but while it is perfectly efficient, queues can be very long and such is the popularity of the Grands Montets that even out of high season there can be a significant wait. As an alternative - if you can put up with the cold - the left-hand queue in the main valley floor station leads to the 11 minute Plan Joran chairlift. The wait at the bottom is always shorter - along with the cold and the time it takes, when you get to the top you then have to take another lift before you can do any skiing. But if you want to avoid standing around, that's the way to do it.

but if there hasn't been a fall in a while the entire distance is likely to unpleasantly moguled. Whatever the conditions, it is worth the queue at the bottom and the bumps at the top simply to ski down alongside the Argentière glacier, a view comparable to anything on the Vallée Blanche. If you want to ski the blacks aware that you'll need patience - the Grands Montets cable car has a permanent queue at the bottom. You will more than likely have to wait for 30 minutes or more before you head up. In addition to this you have to buy a ticket for every journey - available from the kiosk at the mid-station (➥ lift passes).

off-piste
The off-piste options are almost limitless, and in addition to the huge open spaces Les Grands Montets is also home to the Glacier d'Argentière and the Pas de Chevre (➥ off-piste & touring). For those simply wanting powder, the area is so large that even days after a fall there will be fresh tracks to be made somewhere. For bumps skiers, the routes between the pistes become moguled very quickly, and unless there's been a heavy snowfall you can ski on nothing but bumps all day if you feel so inclined.

eating & drinking
Les Grands Montets has a number of choices for **lunch**. Of the restaurants covered below, Lognan and Plan Joran can be very busy and the others are

somewhat out of the way - if you want to avoid the queues without the risk of getting lost, you can ski down to the base station, where there are 2 restaurants and a bar, all of which are perfectly acceptable.

The mid-station has a large restaurant - the **lognan** (t 0450 541021) - on 2 levels: downstairs is self-service, upstairs is very average table service. Outside there is a snack bar, and your best option may be to buy a *sandwiche mixte* and get in the queue for the cable car up. There are sun-loungers outside the restaurant section, where you can picnic if you want.

The **plan joran** (t 0450 541021) is considered by some to be the best mountain restaurant in the valley, and offers a far more ambitious menu than you will find anywhere else. The food is comparable to the better quality places in town - the difference comes in the speed of the table service, which as with most mountain restaurants can be painfully slow. But it does offer a superb range of cuisine and some mouth-watering desserts, and when it is good, it is very good.

Difficult to get to and even more difficult to get away from, the **chalet refuge de lognan** (t 0660 168633) is not ideally placed. You reach it either from the bottom of the Point de Vue run (from the top of the Grands Montets cable car) or by traversing over from the top of the Herse chairlift. Either way you will have worked up an appetite by the time you arrive. It is a small and homely restaurant, away from the masses and with a beautiful view of the glacier. Be warned though - there is no piste leading away from the hut, so you will either have to hike back up the track you came down, or take on a tricky traverse down to the Lognan mid-station or to the red run back to Argentière.

The inventively named **snack bar 3300** is at the top of the Grands Montets cable car, attractive mainly because you can eat your lunch on the roof terrace. Great views, standard food.

la crémerie du glacier (t 0450 540752) is an excellent and very out of the way restaurant, specialising in local food. By late season you can reach the Crémerie by road, but when everything is still snow-covered it is more of a struggle to find. It lies to the right of the red run down to Argentière, at the bottom where the piste intersects with the cross-country route. But blink at the wrong moment and you'll miss it.

If you would rather DIY, there are a couple of **picnic** spots. As you come out of the Bochard bubble, hike up the spike straight in front of you. The view in any direction is fabulous, and right below you is a more-or-less sheer drop down to the Pas de Chevre. Few people

venture up there, because it looks like the start of a scary off-piste run (it's not - though you could technically join the Pas de Chevre from here, you'd need very good snow cover and to be a very, very good skier). If you want to eat indoors, Plan Joran has a picnic room or you can eat outside on the loungers by the Lognan restaurant.

Behind the cable car base station, at the bottom of the run down, there are 2 restaurants and a bar (with a live band every afternoon) - all of which provide good quality **après**. Away from the slopes, the town of Argentière has its own après scene (➞ argentière).

73

bad weather
Les Grands Montets gets more than its fair share of bad weather. Clouds seem to be attracted to the ski area, and often when the rest of the valley is in warm sunshine Les Grands Montets will be in a white-out. The sun will usually break through by the afternoon, but until it does there's nothing much to do except wait - though the run back to the valley floor tends to stay below the clouds. Les Grands Montets cable car is invariably the last lift to re-open after a fresh fall - leading to hordes of powder hounds camping out at the Lognan restaurant waiting to catch the first car up.

getting home
In contrast to Le Brévent and La Flégère the cable car down to

Argentière will not be busy until the end
of the season when you can no longer
ski down. If you prefer, you can take
the Plan Joran chair down to avoid
whatever queue there might be.The red
run down to Argentière has good
artificial snow cover, and is open until
very late in the season. It can get
extremely busy at the end of the day,
and the whole run is an accident
blackspot as all levels of skier and
boarder make their way down
what is at times quite a narrow
piste. Nevertheless, it is better
than taking the cable car, and is
in no way difficult as red runs go.

74

On rolling slopes at the head of the valley, Le Tour is the gentle alternative to the rest of the skiing in Chamonix. It is not, however, only for family cruising: much of the best powder and tree skiing is found there, and it is the least busy of the 4 areas by quite a stretch - though on weekends with the influx of locals it can still be pretty hectic.

Being at the top of the valley, the slopes at Le Tour face in a variety of directions. The entire area is wide open and catches sunshine for much of the day, with the exception of the backside down to the Tête de Balme chair, which is mostly shaded by trees. Thanks to its higher bottom altitude, Le Tour spends longer above the snowline and so has better early and late season snow than Le Brévent and La Flégère.

getting there

Walking to Le Tour is not an option. Unless you are staying at the Olympique hotel by the gondola, or in the small town of Montroc, you're on the bus. It's about 15 minutes by car from Chamonix to Le Tour without traffic. At weekends the free car park will be full by 11am, and the overflow is more than a mile away - so get there early. In high season the journey back to Chamonix can take over 45 minutes in the rush hour, so head down early or take lots of sweets with you.

Once you've got there the gondola up to Charamillon is efficient and quieter

map d

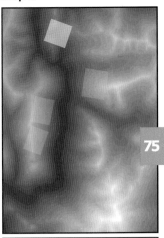

75

snapshot

out of interest
highest point - 2270m
aspect - all
access - gondola
lifts - 2 chairs & 4 drags
pistes - 9 blue, 5 red & 1 black
off-piste - extensive: bowls, trees, itineraries to vallorcine & trient (switzerland)
restaurants - 3

highlights & hotspots
the best tree-skiing in the valley
susceptible to windy conditions
some rarely skied itinerary routes
the col de balme refuge hut

than the other base station lifts. That is not to say that there are never queues, but they are less common and less long than elsewhere in the valley. From the top of the gondola, the Autannes chairlift provides access to the main skiing.

pistes

There are no **green** runs on the mountain - though the Vormaine learners' area alongside Le Tour's gondola provides a home for beginners.

The gentle slopes of Le Tour make for a lot of cruisey **blues**. The majority of the slopes in the area are wide, rolling runs with lots of space for easy turns. One of the highlights of the area is the run leading down through the forest from the Tête de Balme chair to Vallorcine, on the other side of the Col des Montets - but be warned, there is currently no lift to take you back up again. To return to Le Tour you will have either to shuttle cars or take the hourly train to Montroc and catch the bus from there back to the bottom gondola.

As much as the **reds** feel black on La Flégère, they feel blue at Le Tour. There is nothing very steep or narrow in the whole area, and apart from the run down to the Tête de Balme chair, the few reds seem to be there simply to prevent monotony on the piste map. That said, the runs are fun and because of their width are a good place for

beginners to improve or for the more advanced to find their ski legs.

One **black** run is marked on the piste map, but as with the runs from the top of Les Grands Montets it is not actually pisted - it is simply a route down underneath the Tête de Balme chair, and it is a fine place to find powder and good tree-skiing.

off-piste

For anyone not looking for a relaxing day, the reason to go to Le Tour is to find powder. Because almost everyone who heads away from Chamonix after a snowfall goes to Les Grands Montets, fresh snow gets skied out far less quickly at Le Tour. Various large powder bowls are clearly visible and require little or no hiking to reach. The itinerary routes back down to the car park hardly ever get touched, and there is a wealth of open terrain and tree-skiing off the pistes down to the Tête de Balme chair.

eating & drinking

le chalet de charamillon (t 0450 540905) is a large yet cosy restaurant, like the Plan Joran with better views but without the fancy menu. There is a terrace, a large outdoor seating area, and a picnic room on the lower level.

If you want something out of the way and completely different, the **col de balme refuge hut** (t 0450 540233) is your place. It is an authentic refuge, with scant décor, as-it-comes service and an outdoor hole-in-the-floor toilet. There is barely any choice on the menu, but the steak and chips is cheap, and tastes deliciously home-cooked. Also, it is at the end of a flat track - the effort it takes to reach it means it doesn't attract the masses that fill most restaurants. The hut is on the Swiss border, and as well as Euros accepts Swiss Francs should you have any knocking around.

On the red run from the Autannes lift back down to the gondola is a small **snack bar** which isn't marked on the official piste map, and which is easy to miss. As a result it rarely gets too busy, and though the food is simple (and heated in a microwave) it's a great place to sit on a sun-lounger and sip a vin chaud.

For **picnics** the top of the Autannes chair has the best view of the valley - but it can be very windy. At the bottom of the Tête de Balme chair is a sheltered sun-trap that is probably the best spot on a windy day. No one will mind - or even notice - if you picnic at the snack-stop, or alternatively there is a picnic room in the Chalet de Charamillon.

The bar at the Olympique hotel is small and cosy, and has a large terrace for sunny days both of which are suitable for **après**. Aside from that the only option is the tiny buvette at La Vormaine, which is not cosy and which

has a very small 'terrace' for sunny days - but which is usually considerably quieter.

bad weather
When it's windy anywhere in the valley, it's very windy at Le Tour - and therefore also very cold. The tree skiing down to the Tête de Balme chair would make Le Tour an excellent place to go in poor visibility, but more often than not the windspeed will close the access lifts and you won't be able to get there. In short, Le Tour is probably best avoided unless it's sunny.

getting home
The red run under the gondola is as unthreatening as the other reds at Le Tour, and is open right up to the end of the season. After a few broad turns you come to a long final schuss under the gondola that is a fantastic way to end your day's skiing. If you don't fancy the ski down you can take the gondola. There is rarely - if ever - a queue to go down.

77

If the weather isn't doing you any favours, or if you need some ideas about where to head for something specific, below is a bit of location advice.

the first morning
While the valley's most gentle slopes are at Le Tour, you probably don't want to spend your first morning (and your first evening) stuffed in a bus. Save the journey up the valley for the middle of the week - when there will be fewer people - and get your ski legs back on Le Brévent, which has plenty of wide blue space and enough variety for you to build up your confidence without getting bored.

in poor snow
When there's not much skiing to be done, head for Les Grands Montets. It is the highest of the 4 areas, and the north facing slopes hold the snow for longer than anywhere else in the valley. The pistes are the first to open at the start of the season, and the last to close - normally staying open into early May. If it's the middle of the season and it hasn't snowed for a long time, most of the area is likely to be very much a mogul field, but the pistes will still be pistes, and while the snow may be icy in the morning and/or slushy in the afternoon, anything is better than no snow at all.

in bad weather
When the weather closes in, the ChamSki pass has little to offer. 1 or 2 of the lower lifts on La Flégère may be open, but basically in poor visibility there's not much to be done. If you must have a day's skiing, Les Houches at the bottom of the valley is under the tree-line, as is Italy's Courmayeur, just the other side of the Mont Blanc tunnel and closer than you might think. However, Les Houches is only covered by the Mont-Blanc pass, and though a ChamSki pass of 4 days (or longer) gives you a free day in Courmayeur, the tunnel will set you back €40 just to get there.

a good lunch
While the Col de Balme refuge hut at Le Tour is an interesting experience, the only place you'll find memorable food on the mountain is on Les Grands Montets. Plan Joran offers an excellent menu and some mouth-watering desserts if you don't mind waiting for your meal, or if you're feeling adventurous the Chalet Refuge de Lognan serves good food and is away from the pistes in the shadow of the Argentière glacier - but it takes a bit of getting back from. For something that takes a bit of getting to, the Crémerie du Glacier serves perhaps the most hearty (and non-touristy) lunch available - if you can find it (➜ les grands montets).

a mid-week change of pace
If there's been a fresh snowfall, or if after 3 or 4 days your enthusiasm for

steeps and moguls is starting to wane, a day at Le Tour can provide the perfect antidote. You will be hard pressed to find a single bump in the whole area, and most of the pistes are wide and gentle. There are great views back down the valley to Chamonix, some beautiful runs through the trees down to the Tête de Balme chair and Vallorcine, and lunch is available from - amongst other places - an authentic refuge hut, which is a far cry from your standard mountain restaurant.

a bumpy ride

If you like your moguls, Les Grands Montets is unbeatable. The top cable car leads to the famous Point de Vue and Pylons runs, neither of which are pisted and both of which, unless there is fresh powder, will be mogulled for almost their entire length. They are both steep and sustained descents, and there is no backing out once you've started - but if that doesn't sound like you, Les Grands Montets also has moguls to suit every other appetite. The Chamois black run from the Bochard bubble is steep but has a relief track, and the whole area gets skied so much that everywhere on the mountain there are bump runs, of varying gradients and so suited to varying ability levels.

one for the kids?

Because the valley's pisted areas are unlinked there may well not be enough variety to keep the more discerning child entertained for a whole day - and unless your children are competent skiers, there is little to recommend away from Le Tour. As for the Vallée Blanche, youngsters are often unimpressed by its beauty - especially if they've lost their sense of humour on the arête - and queues to get there and to get back probably won't go down too well with anyone who has got a short attention span. Not an easy choice.

to get away from it all

Even when the resort isn't too busy, the valley's pisted areas are small enough that escaping for a bit of peace and quiet can be a difficult thing to do. If you want to see a mountainside that isn't covered in skiers, the best thing to do is to go ski-touring. Hire a guide to take you on the mini-tour over the Col de Berard and down to Le Buet, and the chances are you will barely see another group for most of the day. To do this, however, you need to be a competent skier (comfortable on black runs or off-piste), you need to be in reasonable physical shape, and you'll need to hire touring skis. If you're a boarder, the same trip is possible, using snowshoes where a skier would use skins (→ off-piste & touring).

While the valley's pisted areas are steep and challenging, Chamonix's reputation comes almost entirely from its off-piste skiing. It boasts the justifiably renowned Vallée Blanche, much of the best known and most dangerous extreme skiing in the Alps, and is the launching point for numerous ski-tours including the original haute route. What follows is a description of some of Chamonix's better known routes - none of which should attempted without a guide. For a full description of Chamonix's off-piste see the dual-language book Chamonix Hors-Piste, by François Burnier and Dominique Potard, available from most bookstores in Chamonix.

the vallée blanche

Every year, people from all over the world come to Chamonix just to ski the Vallée Blanche. Its length varies depending on whose description you read, but at roughly 20km from the Aiguille du Midi back down to Chamonix, and with a vertical drop of almost 3000m, it is the longest lift-accessed glacier run in the world. The views are quite unforgettable, and there is skiing to suit all levels of ability from intermediate upwards. Anyone who is comfortable in a controlled snowplough turn can get down the classic route - for boarders accurate control of tight turns is required. The attraction is not how or what you are skiing, but where. The Vallée Blanche has become something that skiers 'do' in the same way as

tourists 'do' Paris or 'do' Rome. The scenery is quite astounding - aside from the hundreds of other skiers, it is an almost otherworldly experience. If you have never strayed out of sight of a lift or a piste marker before, you will not believe your eyes. The descent is on a vast expanse of snow between 2 towering lines of mountains, between seracs (huge blocks of glacial ice) and over snow-bridges that span deep crevasses. Aside from the Requin Hut halfway down (and ignoring all the other people), there is no sign of civilisation. For the recreational skier it is an experience you will never forget.

However, it is high-altitude glacier skiing, and it should not be approached lightly. People die on the Vallée Blanche every year - and almost all accidents happen because of poor preparation or overconfidence. Unless you are proficient on and well equipped for crevassed terrain, you must go with a guide.

getting ready

In the high mountain environment the weather can change from warm sunshine to freezing white-out in a matter of minutes. It can be as cold as -30°C on the Aiguille du Midi, and sunshine down in town is no guarantee of good weather on the mountain. You should take a warm skiing hat, good gloves, goggles as well as sunglasses, a fleece to wear under your skiing clothes... you may need none of this,

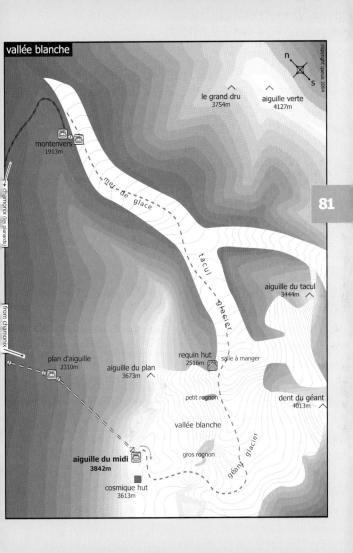

vallée blanche

81

copyright qanuk 2004

n
s

le grand dru
3754m

aiguille verte
4127m

montenvers
1913m

chamonix (les planards)

from chamonix

mer de glace

tacul glacier

aiguille du tacul
3444m

plan d'aiguille
2310m

aiguille du plan
3673m

requin hut
2516m

salle à manger

petit rognon

dent du géant
4013m

vallée blanche

aiguille du midi
3842m

gros rognon

géant glacier

cosmique hut
3613m

but better to bring it than to rue the decision not to. This is the first of a number of reasons to go with a backpack - though if you have never skied with one before, you should be aware that it significantly changes your centre of gravity and so until you adjust to it you may find your balance is a little off.

The Vallée Blanche is busy enough that you need to reserve places on the cable car if you want to ski it in the morning. Your guide will take care of this - you just need to remember your lift pass. If you are going without a guide, you can book either at the base of the cable car or through an automated telephone reservations line (t 0892 680067).

82

food

You could get from top to bottom in 2 hours if you had to, but it is worth taking your time and you are likely to need to eat at some point. There is a restaurant at the top of the cable car, and the Requin Hut at the halfway stage sells food like any other mountain restaurant. But it is always jammed beyond capacity, and a lot of skiers carry sandwiches with them to eat on the way down. Just past the technical stretch through the Géant icefall (see below), the Salle à Manger (dining room) provides the perfect picnic spot. If you decide not to carry lunch, you would be well advised to carry at least a couple of chocolate bars and a bottle of

water just in case. Even if you don't need them, someone else in your group might do.

safety equipment

In addition to warm clothing and food, you will need an avalanche transceiver and a climbing harness, and each group will need a rope. You ski the whole way down wearing your harness - it's very difficult to get someone out of a crevasse if they're not wearing one. Your guide will provide all the equipment and explain how to use it, and will also carry the rope, which is used on the arête (see below) and which would be used for a crevasse rescue.

the aiguille du midi

At the shoulder of Mont Blanc, the Aiguille du Midi stands 3842m high. There is little danger of suffering from altitude sickness at this height, but coming from ground level the air is thin enough to make you short of breath if you try to exercise - if you're sceptical then try running up the stairs to the terrace. Given what it is standing on, the construction is very impressive, and the views from the Midi alone are worth the trip.

the arête

The descent begins with the notorious hike down the arête - about 100m of stepping down a narrow path with a steep drop-off on one side and a very steep drop-off on the other. The north face of the Aiguille du Midi is a 45° convex slope - which gives you a humbling perspective on how shallow even black runs are by comparison. As you stand at the top of it, it feels like 60°. You may not believe it as you look down, but people ski off it.

If you are scared of heights, you won't like it much, but in reality it is not at all dangerous. People have fallen from the

path - and if you fall unroped you are unlikely to survive - but if you are with a guide you will be wearing a climbing harness, and will be roped up to everyone else in your group - so if you slip you won't slip far. Conditions on the path are very variable, and when it's icy, ski boots don't grip very well. Boarders have it easier here, as the rubber soles of boarding boots cope a little better with ice. Wearing crampons makes this climb a simple walk - ask your guide the day before if you are at all concerned.

83

There is a rope on either side of the path to help you balance - but carrying skis and poles it can all become a bit of a panic, especially given the large numbers of people trying to get down at busy times. Another reason to bring a backpack is that if you can attach your skis or board to it, your hands will be much freer to help you climb down.

skis on!

Once you have cleared the arête you reach a small flat area where you can put on your skis or board. This is the launching point for every descent. Unless it has snowed recently, the initial section is likely to be unpleasantly mogulled, but after 50m or so the run flattens out and you are away. 95% of skiers take the classic route down the glacier - if you are in a group of very able skiers there are all sorts of other ways down that are more challenging, and which will have better snow and fewer people. A couple of minutes skiing will be enough for your guide to decide which route is best for you.

the classic route

On a clear day you will share the valley with hundreds of other skiers and boarders, and it can feel like a busy piste. The classic route is shown on the Vallée Blanche map as a dashed red line. Apart from crossing the Seracs du Géant, the whole descent is like a very wide blue run - but don't let this fool you into straying away from the path your guide takes. The entire run is on a glacier, and crevasses can be difficult to spot unless you know what you are looking for. You should never ski below your guide, or more than 10 yards or so either side of the route your guide takes. A simple bump may conceal a gaping hole.

the seracs du géant

About half-way down, the classic route meets the Géant icefall. This is the most impressive part of the descent, and the most challenging section of the skiing. It is basically like a nasty mogul field - it is not very steep, but the bumps are often ledgy. It is essential here that you follow your guide's tracks precisely, turning exactly where your guide turns. You are within feet of crevasses on either side, and you are skiing between huge blocks of glacial ice. Take your camera.

back to chamonix

After following the Mer de Glace down

from the Salle à Manger, the return to town is either by skiing down to join the slopes of Les Planards, or by taking the Montenvers train. Skiing down involves climbing up from the tip of the Mer de Glace over the brow to a small buvette where you can buy food and drink, and then heading on down on a cat-track through the woods. It is narrow and winding, but flat enough to be a simple ski. If there is not enough snow you can take the Montenvers cable car up to the train station. You need your lift pass to use the train.

guides on the vallée blanche

Most Chamonix guides get most of their business from taking groups down the Vallée Blanche, and for them the classic route can become monotonous. If you simply want to ski, just follow your guide down the hill. But if you have any interest in your surroundings, your guide will know the area inside out. If you want to see a huge crevasse from a safe distance, or if you want to know anything about off-piste skiing, most guides will be more than happy to oblige. Similarly if there is anything you are uncomfortable with, just ask - on the whole they are a very friendly and approachable bunch (➜ lessons & guiding).

for boarders

On the classic route there are long flat sections where you may run out of speed, especially if there is a lot of fresh powder. Though you probably

84

won't need them, it is a good idea to take hiking or ski poles so you can help yourself along - another good reason to take a backpack. This is especially true if the other people in your group are skiers, as they will probably stop on sections where it will be difficult for you to pick up speed. If you are unsure, ask your guide before you leave.

beating the crowds

The Vallée Blanche is such an attraction that it is likely to be very busy even during low season. You will not catch the first lift by getting there early in the morning - by 7:30am the cable car station is heaving with skiers, climbers and mountaineers. There are ways to avoid the crowds - but they require a bit of forward planning. One way is to take the last cable car up in the afternoon (at about 4pm) and to stay the night in the Cosmiques Hut, a short traverse from the Aiguille du Midi. The views of the sunset are extraordinary, and staying in a mountain refuge hut is an experience in itself. The following morning you can head down the glacier in perfect quiet, with just the morning sun to keep you company. One word of warning though - sleeping at altitude and thus in thinner air often affects how easily people sleep, so your night's rest may not be entirely restful.

other options

If the arête isn't your cup of tea, or if you want to avoid the queuing before you even get onto the cable car, it is also possible to ski the Vallée Blanche from the Italian side. Through the Mont Blanc tunnel you can reach the base station in little over 20 minutes, and there is rarely much of a queue at the bottom of the lift. There is no arête to hike, the top section of the skiing is likely to have much better snow conditions, and you can enjoy an authentic Italian pasta lunch at the mid-station restaurant before you leave. Just remember your Gucci sunglasses.

glacier d'argentière

85

If you've ever seen it, you'll know that not much skiing takes place actually on the Argentière glacier. It is an extraordinary series of gaping crevasses, and is much better looked at than stepped on. Skiing is possible alongside the glacier - the Point de Vue run from the top of the Grands Montets cable car takes you within spitting distance of the lower section, and with a guide you can descend straight down to the glacier and ski along the left bank, or take various other routes down away from the piste markers.

the pas de chevre

Often fondly mistranslated as the 'No Goats', the Goat Step is a steep and scary couloir descent, which you can't opt out of once you have started. Don't even consider the Pas de Chevre unless you are an expert skier, and no matter how good you are don't try it without a guide. There are 3 couloirs from the top of the Grands Montets cable car west down to the Mer de Glace. They are all steep, and they are all technically very demanding. Route finding in the bottom section can be extremely difficult if there is poor snow cover. But if you have the ability and the guts, the Pas de Chevre will be one of the experiences of your life.

ski touring

There is a whole world of skiing that goes almost unnoticed by the majority of recreational skiers. Those used to huge, linked ski areas with endless lifts and mile after mile of pisted runs may well not know what ski touring is. It is also called ski mountaineering, which is perhaps a more appropriate name for it - it consists effectively of climbing up mountains before skiing down them. It is quite unlike normal skiing in that it is entirely off-piste, and 'tours' consist of travelling from 'a' to 'b' in the same way as hiking trails in summer.

Obviously to make this possible a lot of different equipment is necessary. To climb up slopes with skis on you need touring bindings, which you can unlock to allow your heel to come away from the ski as you step upwards. You also carry 'skins' - so called because they were originally seal skins - which are strips attached to the bottom of the ski during a climb to allow them to slip uphill but prevent them from sliding down. For many tours it is also necessary to be proficient with climbing

ropes and harnesses... but as with most things in Chamonix, if you hire a guide you will be surprised what you can do - and all these delights are available to boarders as well, simply using snowshoes or approach skis when skiers use skins.

Chamonix is the perfect place to start ski touring - and few people that try it ever look at piste skiing in the same way again. A short route from the top of the Cornu lift (in Le Brévent area) via the Col de la Glière down to the Combe Lachenal (in La Flégère area) combines a good introduction to skinning with a short but sweet powder run.

An excellent start to true touring is the mini-tour over the Col de Berard. The route starts on La Flégère and finishes in the small town of Le Buet, out of the top of the valley on the other side of the Col de Montets. The first half of the tour involves an hour or 2 of hiking and skinning, split into 2 sections by a 10 minute traverse. The second half is a beautiful 1-2 hour descent from the Col de Berard along the line of the Eau de Berard river, which by mid April will be melted and flowing. You are unlikely to see many other people, as the tour is a way off the beaten track. From Le Buet there is an hourly train service back to Chamonix - the station is just over the road from the hotel and bar where the tour ends. The best map that covers the route is the IGN (the French OS) hiking map number 3630OT, a 1:25000 scale topographical map available from any of the bookstores in town.

the haute route

The 'high level road' from Chamonix to Zermatt takes 6 days to complete, crossing more than 20 glaciers and with some 10000m of combined ascent and descent. It was first skied in the early 20th century, and though many other haute routes have since been

established this is the original, now known as the 'classic' haute route.

The route can of course be done in reverse, from Zermatt to Chamonix, but the majority of parties travel from west to east, starting above Argentière at the top of the Grands Montets cable car, and via a number of variations finishing in Zermatt under the north face of the Matterhorn. The nights are spent in refuge huts - small buildings dotted around the mountains which provide evening meals, basic sleeping space, and an escape from cold and inclement weather.

It will make very real demands on your skiing and on your personal fitness, and it should not be undertaken without considerable preparation. The reward is outstanding skiing in some of the most beautiful mountain scenery in the world, making your way through high-alpine backcountry from Mont Blanc to the Matterhorn. Europe's mountains offer nothing better.

For a full description of the route, see Peter Cliff's book The Haute Route, published by Cordee and available from most bookstores in Chamonix.

Chamonix's jagged mountains provide the perfect forum for extreme competitions. There are also a number of smaller events that are not swamped by professionals - so if you've perfected that 360 and fancy your chances, read on...

Now sadly departed, the ChamJam (i chamjam.com) was the staple of the Chamonix events calendar. The week long fiesta was ousted after 'complications' at the 2003 event, and has relocated to Soldeu-El Tartar in Andorra. In its place there is currently nothing, but the event licence still exists and Les Grands Montets snowpark needs an excuse to be groomed. Something will fill the gap, and sooner rather than later.

The **bosse des bosses** is an inter-resort race down a specially prepared mogul run (with a jump at the end) on Les Grands Montets. The Bosse des Bosses used to be part of the ChamJam but now features as a stand-alone event in mid-March, which gives seasonnaires the excuse they need to congregate in Chamonix for a short ski and a long drinking session. The rivalry between resorts is intense (though friendly), and the standard at the top end is very impressive - many of the entrants are sponsored riders who happen to live in the relevant resorts. Marks are awarded for speed and style. Only skiers need apply.

The **o'neill extreme** is a 'watch-only' event, which takes place around the mid-season mark. The cream of the world's free-skiers show off their skills on a steep and rocky off-piste course. They are marked on speed, style, and difficulty of line - and the ability of the competitors has to be seen to be believed. The viewing point is the finish post, where the sponsors set up a food stall, and it makes a perfect place for a lazy lunch in the sunshine. Location is normally Le Brévent - but look out for posters around town to confirm the details.

The **winter ride** is a freeride contest that covers the length of the valley and the duration of the season. Though organisation changes from year to year, typically there will be 1 event per month or so, starting in January and culminating in a final towards the end of the season. Each event has a different location - so one on Le Brévent, one on La Flégère and so on. Effectively the organisers just pick an off-piste line and the competitors have to get from top to bottom as fast as possible. The event is as much social as it is competitive, and the majority of entrants are locals or seasonnaires. It's very much a loud music and experimental hairstyles occasion, and typical to the seasonnaire community the atmosphere is young, vibrant, and carefree.

The Chamonix leg of the **World Cup downhill** takes place on the Kandahar run at Les Houches, a short drive down the valley from Chamonix. The event is usually in early January - information on the exact time is readily available on the internet and in ski magazines. Les Houches is not covered by the ChamSki pass, so you'll have to buy a separate day-pass to watch from the mountainside, but it will be well worth the money - seeing racers shoot past you at Ski Sunday speeds is something not to be missed.

There are various smaller events during the season, organised by the ESF or by local sponsors. Les Planards just on teh edge of the town plays host to a number of evening displays under floodlights, including a big air display towards the end of the season. Events like these will be advertised on flyers and posters around town.

89

If you need a break from the downhill grind, there are plenty of other things to keep you entertained on the snow.

Ski de Fond (**cross-country skiing**) has a special place in Chamonix life - many locals who are not so excited about the hordes of high-speed skiers on the pistes enjoy the snow in the relative quiet of the valley floor's extensive network of cross-country pistes, which are open 9am-5pm every day of the season. Chamonix (t 0450 531115) and Argentière (t 0450 541422) have a number of circuits, and throughout the winter the golf course in Les Praz functions as a multi-activity area. The valley has a total of about 70km of pistes. The spread out lift systems also means that there is an enormous area available for **snowshoeing**. Most of the guiding companies offer snowshoe trips - most popularly on the Mer de Glace, though with a guide you can go pretty much anywhere you want.

Though **heliskiing** is illegal in France, you can make drops in neighbouring Italy or more expensively in Switzerland. Chamonix Mont-Blanc Hélicoptères (t 0450 541382) will organise trips for you as will the guiding companies, and as with on the Vallée Blanche, the cost of the trip covers everything you need, including avalanche transceivers.

If you've ever fancied being pulled along by a train of **huskies**, you can try

it in Chamonix - either for 20 or 30 minutes as a passenger or on an hour-long instruction course at the end of which you should be able to control the sled on your own. Surprisingly, it is not so much exciting as relaxing, as the sled doesn't exactly reach break-neck speeds. Evolution 2 offer the husky experience, as do Husky Dalen (t 0450 477724/0684 993467), a husband and wife team who operate next to the learners' slopes at La Vormaine.

On Thursday nights, Les Houches opens the floodlit lower section of a piste for free **night-skiing**. It is basically a promotional venture to raise the profile of the resort - but there's vin chaud on offer, and even skiing a gentle slope is a pretty different experience under lights.

Trips up the **aiguille du midi** or the **montenvers train** are more about seeing the snow than being active on it. The cable car ride up the Aiguille is expensive, but the trip is unforgettable. If you are not going to ski, go at lunchtime or later, when there will be no queue. The Montenvers train takes you up to the Mer de Glace, the finish point for the Vallée Blanche ski run. There is an ice grotto carved out of the glacier containing some rather incongruous ice sculptures and displays, but the trip is made worthwhile far more by the scenery. The 'attractions' are enough to keep young children entertained, but it reeks of tourism - the Aiguille is a far more impressive experience.

snapshot

manna for boarders

For a long time a snowpark was conspicuously absent from Cham's otherwise comprehensive list of attractions. There is now, at last, one worthy of the resort. Located down in Les Bossons (320 Route de Tissières t 0450 531239, open 12-4:30pm, 7-10pm), on the valley floor and driving distance from the middle of town, it is both a struggle to get to and subject to a rather shorter season than the rest of the skiing. But aside from that, there is little to complain about. It's a decent sized park with lines of rails and jumps for all levels ability. 2 minutes'

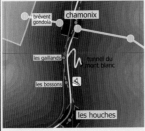

worth of draglift will have you back at the top of the park, and often (especially in the evenings) you will have the park largely to yourself.

There's not much in the way of big air - the slope isn't very steep, so there's only 1 large jump at the bottom of the run, but this lack of gradient works very much in the park's favour for all but the best riders: one of the most off-putting things about jumping can be a steep landing. If you aren't sure you're going to have your board (or skis) under you when you hit the snow, in this park you know the worst that can happen is you'll bang your backside a bit, whereas in other places you run the risk of bouncing your way down a hefty slope before you come to a halt.

That said, there's still plenty of potential to hurt yourself here, especially off some of the rails. Appropriate safety equipment is advised - though entirely optional. Helmets and padding may save you a concussion or a broken coccyx, but for some people they don't look so cool. The choice is yours.

There's also a workshop and test centre, live DJing some evenings, and a bar to give your girlfriend somewhere to drink vin chaud while you're outside falling over. Tickets are available by the session, or if you think you'll be back you can buy a 10 session ticket or a season pass.

the resort

eating out

Nowhere is the variety on offer in Chamonix more evident than in its choice of eateries. There are countless cafés, take-aways, boulangeries, pâtisseries and more than 50 restaurants... in numerous different incarnations - modern European style, a huge selection of traditional Savoyarde places serving steaks, fondues and raclette, and also Italian, Chinese, Japanese, Indian, Mexican... there is even a McDonald's. In fact there is a gross overpopulation of Savoyarde restaurants. Most are much the same as

94

each other, offering similar menus and similar service in similarly touristy 'traditional' surroundings. None are particularly bad, but some stand out as being particularly good. The reviews are not intended to be comprehensive - rather they cover the best of what is on offer, both in town and around the valley.

restaurants

Most restaurants close 1 evening during the week, usually Monday or Tuesday. Wednesday is traditionally the chalet staff night off, and so is the busiest night of the week for restaurants, so it is a good idea to book well in advance. Some restaurants operate on a 2-sitting basis, with the first sitting around 7 or 7:30pm, and the second around 9 or 9:30pm. They are usually quite relaxed about you arriving late or overstaying the first sitting, but in many places you won't be able to book a table for 8pm.

snapshot

April 2006

for something...
at breakfast - atelier café *lunch*
cheap - eldorado
cheesy - crémerie paccard
reassuringly expensive - le chaudron
reassuringly good - munchie
late - belouga
meaty - le carlina
romantic - l'atmosphère
by the river - grand central

prices

The featured restaurants are differentiated by the grading £-£££££ reflecting the approximate price per head for a main course excluding drinks. Price is not an indication of quality - all of the reviewed restaurants are in our opinion worth a visit. The price ranges are as follows:
£ under €8
££ €8-14
£££ €15-22
££££ €23-30
£££££ over €30
All featured restaurants accept most major credit cards.

copyright ⓒanuk 2004

95

restaurants

1 le carlina
2 la bergerie
3 le pitz
4 le chaudron
5 gecko
6 le sanjon
7 l'imprevu
8 l'impossible
9 l'atmosphere
10 bumble bee
11 le caveau
12 munchie
13 maison carrier
14 satsuki
15 la spiga d'oro
16 eldorado
17 le tetras
18 le dragon d'or
19 poppadum's
20 annapuna
21 mcdonald's

le carlina   ££££

☎ 0450 531898
🕐 11am-11pm
🍴 traditional savoyarde

A superbly friendly place right in the centre of town. Le Carlina has a huge menu of steaks and fondues that are all deliciously well prepared, and served with expert off-hand professionalism. The restaurant is in quite a large open plan area and does not look like a traditional local restaurant - but if you want an authentically French experience then you are better off here than in some of the other local Savoyarde restaurants that spend more effort keeping up appearances.

Unusually, they do not take reservations so you will always be able to get a table, and normally with no more than a 5 or 10 minute wait - though if you are in a large group it is worth calling ahead to warn them. If you do end up sitting at the bar for a bit, you can drink your pre-dinner beers out of litre-sized glasses, which are big enough to make you light-headed simply by looking at them.

Le Carlina is open all day, so if you're taking a day away from the slopes you can indulge yourself in a big lunch, or while away your lazy afternoon snacking on food or sipping coffee on the large riverside terrace.

<< in town >>

le chaudron £££

p95
f3

☏ 0450 534034
🕐 6pm-11pm
🍴 traditional savoyarde

A small and cosy spot on the Rue des Moulins, the Cauldron squeezes traditional Savoyarde excellence into minute surroundings. It is a family run restaurant offering the range of fondues you will find everywhere else as well as a decent range of duck and steak - but all presented with a much more personal and professional touch. This is not a place to go to in a large group, as the room can take no more than 30 diners, but if you want good food, intimate surroundings, and friendly attentiveness - and if you don't mind paying a bit more than the average for your cheese - Le Chaudron is one of the best choices in town.

le pitz £££

p95
f2

☏ 0450 530508
🕐 12pm-11pm
🍴 pizza & savoyarde

Unfortunately named, Le Pitz is in fact a very friendly and welcoming pizzeria that also serves all the Savoyarde specialities along with a variety of crêpes and other sweet things. It is open from lunchtime onwards, and has a bar and a large heated terrace where you can sip your

snapshot

in tartiflette we trust...
Chamonix is nestled in the Haute Savoy, a region with a strong tradition for local cuisine. Though you can find pretty much any kind of food in the valley, more than half of the restaurants specialise in the regional dishes of fondue (meat or cheese), raclette (a dish made purely from melted cheese, normally served with potatoes) and tartiflette (layers of potatoes mixed with cheese and crème fraîche, cooked in a massive wok-style pan).

97

Savoyarde food is a long way removed from the French chic of nouvelle cuisine - the portions are large, and there's no fitting them into a low-carbohydrate diet. Fortunately, the high altitude and low temperatures of the mountains mean that your body burns a lot more fat than usual - so rather than making you put on weight, the stodginess of the food is what will keep your muscles going through 6 days of hard skiing and keep you warm when the temperatures dip into minus figures.

vin chaud. The roadside setting isn't quite as charming as the pedestrianised town centre, but if you need something as soon as you get off the bus, or if you feel like going somewhere a little bit away from the crowds on the main drag, Le Pitz could be your place.

eating out

le gecko £££

☎ 0450 533557
🕐 12pm-11pm
🍴 traditional savoyarde & pizza

As much a bar as it is a restaurant, and about as casual as they come. Open all day - and hence an excellent spot for lunch if you are learning on the Savoy slope - and quieter all day than most places thanks to its being a short distance from the centre. The menu is mostly steak and fondue, with a vegetarian option, all very reasonably priced and all as tasty as you will find anywhere else. Gecko has very welcoming French ownership, a très petite terrace, and a number of small TVs (which show mostly Eurosport, so don't go hoping for English football).

l'impossible ££££

☎ 0450 532036
🕐 7pm-11pm
🍴 traditional savoyarde

By reputation one of the best Savoyarde restaurants in Chamonix. L'Impossible is based in a large converted farmhouse on the outskirts of Cham Sud, which creates a warm cosy feel in spite of its size. There is a sense here that the staff take pride in their food and service that is missing in some of the more central Savoyarde restaurants. The menu offers a comprehensive range of everything you would expect to find, and the food is

98

every bit as good as it sounds. Its only drawback is that is not in the centre of town - but it is right next to the Jekyll (➥ après-ski & nightlife) and there is parking across the road.

la crémerie paccard ££££

☎ 0450 531387
🕐 7:30pm-11pm
🍴 traditional savoyarde

A lovely and authentic restaurant attached to the Hermitage Paccard (➥ hotels). It is a large place with a very different décor and feel to most restaurants: every detail has been carefully considered and the atmosphere created is friendly and welcoming. The food is equally well presented with a wide range of restaurant specialities - the tartiflette des Aravis is especially recommended, as are the local ice creams for dessert. It is a 5 minute walk from the centre of town and so is not ideally convenient - though it is close to the MBC (➥ après-ski & nightlife).

mcdonald's £

☎ 0450 533113
🕐 8am-11pm
✗ mcdonald's

p95
e3

A high-ceilinged restaurant at the end of the Avenue Michel Croz, McDonald's sells a none-too-healthy range of burgers and chips, chicken and dips, a variety of breakfasts, and these days some salads as well. The décor is an odd mix of plastic and wood, which is a little out of keeping with the usual ski-resort warmth - but though there is also a mass-produced feel to the food, it is curiously appealing. There is a special menu for children, 5 internet stations (though no good coffee)... McDonald's is open all day and does not take reservations - you will rarely have to wait for a table, and the service though often surly is probably the fastest of anywhere in town.

eldorado £

☎ 0450 533123
🕐 11am-11pm
✗ tex-mex

p95
c4

A very informal restaurant on the outskirts of the centre. Eldorado is only a 5 minute walk from most pubs and is equally accessible from Cham Sud. The food is typical tex-mex, tasty and filling, but the main attraction of Eldorado is the relaxed atmosphere. It is an excellent place for a large party or a family, as it has none of the pretensions of grander restaurants and the prices are low enough that the bill won't put you off your lunch the next day. Though the only gold you'll find is in the range of tequila, there is a long bar to slide your shot glass down, 5 internet stations, and it serves omelettes at lunchtime.

maison carrier ££££

☎ 0450 530003
🕐 12pm-2pm, 7pm-9:30pm
✗ french & pig

p95
f/g2

Technically a part of the Albert Première hotel, the Maison Carrier offers a splendid contrast to the excellent but high-priced extravagance of its Michelin-starred big brother. Where the hotel's namesake restaurant is pure gourmet, the Carrier is chalet-style dining for all the family. Attached to the Albert's more rustic 'Hammeau' annex, the theme is carried through to the restaurant, which features beautiful decoration and an informal (though utterly professional) approach to food. Service is friendly and staff are willing to guide you through the selection of wine - you can just chat to your waiter about what would best suit your meal. You will get butter with your pre-meal bread - a rarity in France - and the main menu is filled with hearty cuisine that is entirely un-nouveau. Lots of the dishes contain pig in some incarnation or other: intended to concord with the farm-style theme. It all works, and superbly so.

eating out

munchie £££

☎ 0450 534541
🕐 6pm-11pm
🍴 french

The best restaurant on the Rue des Moulins, serving first class food at reasonable prices. The menus and the presentation are as you would expect to find in a good London restaurant, and there is something for all tastes - and some wonderful desserts for those with a sweet tooth. The service is intelligent and friendly, and its location makes it an ideal place for those with pre- or post-dinner plans. It is on 3 levels: 2 small eating areas separated by a little bar on the middle floor, which tends to be a seasonnaire hangout. The staff are mostly Scandinavian and so along with speaking better French than you they also speak perfect English. As ever, book in advance as Munchie is very popular.

100

bumble bee £££

☎ 0450 535003
🕐 7pm-11pm
🍴 greek, spanish & tapas

A very cosy and informal restaurant at the top of the Rue des Moulins. Bumble Bee is a small English run place and offers a genuinely personal family welcome - if what you want is some-where you can chat to the owners as you eat, this is it. The menu is not as extensive as some larger restaurants but the food is well chosen and expertly prepared, and you will be full when you leave. Tables get booked up quickly, especially for the early evening - and while it's not a big enough place to sit at the bar and wait for a table, given its location you won't be short of alternatives for a pre-dinner drink or two.

la bergerie ££

☎ 0450 534504
🕐 12pm-10pm
🍴 traditional savoyarde

Rather larger inside than you might expect, La Bergerie is one of the best Savoyarde restaurants in the town. It is pleasingly dark and feels genuinely French - especially if you drop in for an afternoon espresso, when you will likely find any number of locals working their way through packets of Gauloises. Seating is divided between booths and normal tables, food is divided between Savoyarde standards and a variety of grilled meats, and though the service can at times be a little divided too, as overall quality goes you are much better off in here than the more commercial attempts at French authenticity.

l'atmosphère ££££

☎ 0450 559797
🕐 7pm-11pm
🍴 french

One of the best restaurants, Atmosphère has impeccable service and a lovely interior with some seating overlooking the river. Centrally located and with an excellent range of choices on the menu, including some outstanding fish dishes (specialities include lobster, grilled seabass fillet and a superb tuna carpaccio). The restaurant is French run and feels slightly formal, but is very welcoming with it. Like many restaurants in Chamonix, Atmosphère runs 2-sittings, the first at around 7:15pm and the second around 9:15pm - though in practice they aren't too officious about the timing. Because of its location it tends to be busy, so it is well worth booking.

le caveau   ££

☎ 0450 558618
🕐 6:30pm-2am
🍴 pizza, swedish & international

p95
e3   11

One of Chamonix's best hidden secrets, in both senses: it is one of the best secrets and one of the best hidden. If you can find it, you will discover a place that is true to its name - it used to be a sheep pen, after which it was a wine and cheese cellar. More recently a nightclub, it now finds itself serving an exhaustive and indefinable array of foods. Amongst other things the surprisingly underpriced menu features the chose-your-own-adventure "mild or wild" pizza, meatballs in the best Swedish tradition and a number of Thai dishes. The cave-like surroundings house mostly booth-style seating, which makes for a noisy yet unobtrusive atmosphere that runs until well into the small hours. In theory you could wander in at 1 in the morning and sit down to eat - or if you're just passing by the pizzas are available to take away.

and the rest...

If none of the above entice, the rest include... 2 indians, the **annapurna** (t 0450 558139) in the centre and **poppadum's** (t 0450 532832) in Cham Sud, for those missing their chicken madras, **le dragon d'or** (t 0450 533725) for a sweet & sour fix, **satsuki** (t 0450 532199) for Japanese specialities, very reasonably priced sushi to eat in or take-away, **la spiga d'oro** (t 0450 530649), a combined shop and restaurant for Italian ingredients and **le tetras** (t 0450 533397) for tex-mex in the heart of Cham Sud. You shouldn't go hungry.

<< further afield >>

la ferme des trois ours ££

☎ 0450 546306
🕐 8am-11pm
🍴 traditional french

A large and very unusual place that, if you can get there, is entirely worth the journey. As the name suggests, it is a farm, and though there are no bears (and no porridge) there are cows and the like lingering on the outskirts of the eating area - so when you order something with cheese in (which is plentiful on the menu) you know where it came from. The open plan layout is warm and smoky, and being in Vallorcine is also very much less touristy than places in Chamonix. The 3 bears opens morning, noon and evening for breakfast, lunch and dinner, and no matter when you go you will find an eating experience that in terms of atmosphere is quite unlike anything in the Chamonix valley.

le robinson ££

☎ 0450 534587
🕐 6pm-10pm
🍴 traditional savoyarde

Chamonix at its most defensively French, this not a place you should visit if your local lingo doesn't stretch past "un table pour deux". In many ways they would rather not be discovered at all - but Francophiles looking for local cheer that doesn't succumb to the commercial heatwave will be well satisfied - as will families needing somewhere to dispense the children after eating as there is a huge garden with various playthings, and beyond that nothing much but trees and snow and the odd cross-country piste. It's cheap and jolly, and along with the Savoyarde favourites offers monstrous portions of *tartiflette* (tartiyak!) and an endlessly cheesy *Croûte Savoyarde* (*Croûte du Yeti*), with free Génépy for those who manage to finish. One of their USPs is their chef, who is openly advertised as being a little grumpy and not much of a talker. You probably get the idea by now - not for everyone, but heaven for some.

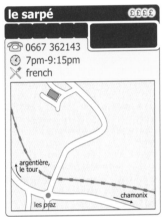

le sarpé ££££

📞 0667 362143
🕐 7pm-9:15pm
🍴 french

For those who know about it, Le Sarpé is a required stop in a visit to Chamonix. Without a car it's not easy to get to, but once you're there you'll know why so many of its customers are regulars: the simple room is abuzz with rustic atmosphere, and it feels as if everybody knows everybody else. Tucked away in Les Bois, it is well away from the noise of Chamonix town - no one could get there accidentally, so you can be sure of being surrounded by people with a common purpose - and surprisingly, clientele is about 70% English, enticed by the excellent foie gras and tagliatelle. Set menus all include a cheese plate, and many of the main dishes are fish based.

The Sarpé is very difficult to fault, and though the upper end of the menu isn't cheap, if you're watching your wallet (or your waistline) there are simple alternatives on offer too.

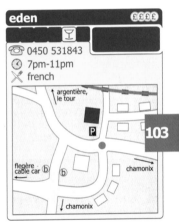

eden ££££

📞 0450 531843
🕐 7pm-11pm
🍴 french

The restaurant in the Eden hotel in Les Praz is in the running for best restaurant in the valley. Set menus range from the very affordable to the menu dégustation at around €80, and all dishes are available à la carte. The beef carpaccio, veal fillet and crème brûlée are especially recommended, but all dishes are tasty, flawlessly prepared and presented by a chef with a real enthusiasm for his food. The restaurant is smartish, but with no obligation to formality, and the service is infallible in both the restaurant and the adjoining bar, which stays open until the last customer leaves.

cafés

If the après in the bars is a little too hectic, or you need a quick recharge before you head into it, Chamonix has various businesses devoted to providing a more relaxed way of life. There are numerous boulangeries and pâtisseries around the town where you can stock up on calories, but if you are looking for something a little different, your options range from coffee and bagels to cheese and fine wines. Most of the cafés are open through the lunchtime siesta, so if you find your shopping trip abruptly cut short at midday when the shops close, they are somewhere to while away the 2 hour break.

104

la crêperie bretonne £

☎ 0450 531604
🕐 11:45am-9:30pm
🍴 crêpes

Although their tag-line of being "the only crêperie in Chamonix" isn't quite true (there's 1 by the hotel Vallée Blanche on Rue du Lyret), this is the pick of the 2. The menu offers a staggering number of galettes (savoury pancakes) with questionable fillings like chicken curry, or sausages and mustard, and a more comfortable range of crêpes (the sweet version) which you'll probably be more inclined to indulge in. The interior feels a little plasticky, but it's a good place to fill up your stomach - and indeed has a very good tartiflette on the set menu.

le bistro des sports £

p105
f3

☎ 0450 530046
🕐 8:30am-11pm
🍴 bar snacks

On Chamonix's busy main street, and generally very French... certainly very local, but entirely welcoming to anyone wanting an espresso and a seat away from the crowds. The Bistro opens early, stays open until the evening, and has a bar in case you need some alcohol to wash down your coffee. Though it is really a café the evenings occasionally involve live local musicians or DJs - which only add to the French ambience. The name is misleading though - don't go here if you're looking for big TV screens to watch the football, because there aren't any.

l'atelier café ££

p105
e3

☎ 0450 523236
🕐 8:30am-7pm April 2006
🍴 cooked breakfast & pm snacks

A good spot for a bacon and egg breakfast, or for Chamonix's best croque monsieur in the afternoon. The Atelier is right in the centre of town, by the river, and the large terrace makes it a perfect spot in good weather. When it's cold outside, the high-ceilinged interior is a warm and welcoming place to round off a day on the slopes without losing your personal space to a horde of beer swilling karaoke experts.

copyright qanuk 2004

105

cafés & take-away

1. l'atelier café
2. le bistro des sports
3. la crêperie bretonne
4. grand central
5. gouthé
6. le lapin agile
7. la potinière
8. belouga
9. cappadoce
10. midnight express
11. poco loco
12. pizza salsa

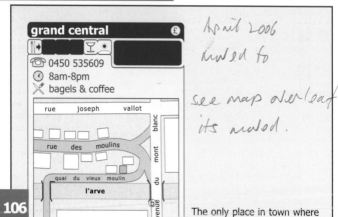

grand central £

☎ 0450 535609
🕙 8am-8pm
🍴 bagels & coffee

April 2006
lined to
see map overleaf
its moved.

106

The only place in town where you can get your latte fix. Unless you like your coffee compressed into a shot mug, Chamonix can be quite frustrating - but Grand Central offers a comprehensive coffee menu alongside a creative list of smoothies and health drinks, and bagels imported from New York and stuffed to the brim with an original and mouth-watering range of fillings.

The interior isn't quite big enough to fit a sofa - this is the coffee shop experience, Chamonix style: down by the river on the edge of the Rue des Moulins, it is the perfect place for an outdoor breakfast under the gaze of Mont Blanc, for a take-away coffee on your way to the Alpina bus stop, or for an afternoon vin chaud and snack on your way into town. Grand Central has a late licence, and from time to time will stay open beyond the advertised 8pm closing time, but whenever you go you will find a personal and genuinely friendly welcome.

Along with offering food to take-away you can also pre-book a packed lunch to take with you up the mountain - just drop in or telephone the day before, and your bagel will be ready wrapped for you as you head off to the slopes in the morning.

la potinière ££

📞 0450 530284
🕐 10am-11pm
🍴 classic french bistro

Better known as 'the Pot', this central eatery on the main square (Place Balmat) is more restaurant than café, and has a full menu which runs throughout the day and into the evening. In addition to numerous 'plat du jour' main courses they serve a selection of salads and a wonderful stringy-cheese French onion soup, and the busy terrace and good-humoured service make it a favourite lunchtime spot when the weather starts to warm up.

le lapin agile ££

📞 -
🕐 11am-11pm
🍴 assiettes of meat & cheese

The Agile Rabbit is a wine bar - one of only 2 in Chamonix - with a vast array of fine wines from around the world. Most can be bought by the glass, and the owner is only too happy to discuss their origins with the discerning drinker - if your French is up to it. To balance your palate, the menu also offers a selection of meats and cheeses and the 3 small private rooms are also available for dinner. All in all a refined and very different experience, in a town that at times can feel a little too touristy or a little too local.

gouthé £

📞 0450 535895
🕐 4pm-7pm
🍴 pâtisserie

On the Rue des Moulins opposite the Bureau des Guides, Gouthé boasts what is possibly the most enticing window display in town. It is a pâtisserie like no other, with a fabulous range of homemade cakes and pastries and a drinks menu which offers - amongst other things - 4 different types of hot chocolate. If you have a weakness for sweet things, Gouthé is one place where you can consume enough calories to keep you skiing for months.

107

late night & take-away

Despite the huge range of restaurants, there are any number of reasons to want take-away. If you fancy eating standing up, or if all the restaurants closed before you got to them, you have plenty of choices for a quick bite at any time of the day and most of the hours of darkness. Surprisingly, nothing stays open after 2am, but until then the centre of town does a bustling trade in burgers and baguettes. Options in Cham Sud are more limited, but wherever you are you're not too far from somewhere that sells hot food until late . If you like the idea of take-away but want someone to bring food to you, Saveurs du Monde (t 0450 471269) deliver from a number of restaurants.

108

excellent and there is a range of 10 or so sauces to go with your choice of food.

A popular take-away joint that specialises in big crusty buns filled with far more chips than burger. The menu is a typical variety of patties and cheeses and fillings and sauces, but something in the hectic ordering process often seems to get lost in the translation. Any attempts at French are likely to be met with an attempt at English... but if what you need is carbohydrate stodge, you can't go far wrong.

The best take-away place in Chamonix. A very wide range of delicious toasted sandwiches, which the option of "steak" (burger), but which are mostly a blend of meats, cheeses and vegetables that feels rather like a Pizza Express menu. Options include Camembert, goats cheese, lamb, jambon cru... you can buy beer should you want to drink on the street, and about halfway through the season when the weather warms up they sell ice creams. Nothing is missing - even the chips are

Just along from Midnight Express, and somewhat better quality unless you like the 'crusty bread filled with chips' approach. Poco Loco sells baguettes and burgers, large helpings of chips, crêpes, and everything else you would expect... and also has extremely friendly ownership, a bar inside and an upstairs eating area - possibly the narrowest one in the world - which has a little TV and is a hangout for locals and some of the younger ESF instructors.

au four à bois   £

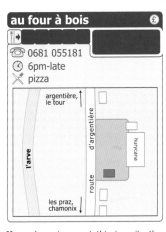

☏ 0681 055181
🕐 6pm-late
✕ pizza

If you have transport this is quite the best way to eat pizza - call ahead and order or simply drive to the parking outside the Hurycana sports shop and see your meal flame-baked in front of you. Given that it only offers pizza, the menu is pretty imaginative and even the bases are exquisitely tasty. In the evening, with no traffic, Au Four à Bois is only 2 minutes from Argentière and 10 minutes from Chamonix, and is well worth the journey.

le garage   £

☏ 0450 536469
🕐 10pm-4am
✕ baguettes

The Garage is a night club, of course, but since there is nowhere to go for food after 2pm, the cloakroom here is the last place where it is available - they stock a basket full of baguettes which they sell as you leave. Don't pass up the opportunity if it's 4am, because you won't find anywhere else open until the boulangeries get going at around 6am.

cappadoce   £

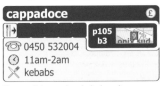

p105
b3

☏ 0450 532004
🕐 11am-2am
✕ kebabs

Chamonix's only kebab shop, though not quite what you might be used to. The Doner meat tastes more or less like meat, which is somehow not entirely satisfying, and the cardboardy pitta bread is rather different to what you get in England. The non-Doner menu is the normal range of chicken and burgers and while the food is uninspiring, if kebabs are your thing this is your only option.

109

pizza salsa   £

p105
e2

☏ 0450 539690
🕐 11am-10:30pm
✕ pizza

One the way to/from Chamonix's new centre of cool, for Elevation, Goophy or Chambre Neuf (➡ après-ski & nightlife) this is your nearest pizza stop. There's no indoors, but everything happens quickly, so you won't have to stand around in the cold for too long while you wait.

après-ski & nightlife

Chamonix has the most diverse and perhaps the liveliest après-ski in the Alps. This is basically thanks to the size of the place - it has more than 30 bars (not including hotel bars), the majority of which open at 4pm and stay open until 1 or 2 in the morning. Whatever your taste may be, with a bit of effort you will find something in Chamonix to keep you happy. Any men looking for holiday romance need to be careful - the valley has a reputation for having the highest male to female ratio in the Alps, and there certainly are some bars where you will be hard pushed to spot a girl in the throng of drinkers.

bars & pubs

The majority of the bars are run and staffed by ex-pats and seasonnaires from **english** speaking countries - and anyone working in a bar will be able to speak enough English to take your order. That's not to say that you shouldn't try to speak the language if you can, but the chances are that you'll be talking to someone who would understand you better in your native tongue.

Chamonix is big enough that there isn't really a timetable to the week. Almost every night is busy somewhere - the only exception being Saturday evenings which thanks to being the first night of most people's holiday is rather unpredictable - arriving seems to inspire either mass hysteria or utter lethargy,

> ### snapshot
>
> **après...**
> beer - mbc
> cheer - elevation 1904
> atmosphere - chambre neuf
>
> **après après...**
> english chill - cybar
> french chic - l'expédition
> swedish beauty - south bar
>
> **and dawn-breakers**
> party people - dicks tea-bar
> true clubbing - l'arbate
> cosy cool - cantina

and accordingly the pubs and clubs are either hugely busy or completely deserted. Wednesday is typically the chalet night off, but as fewer than half of Chamonix's seasonnaires work in chalets this is no reason to expect town to be significantly busier than usual.

prices

You should expect to pay €10ish for a pitcher of beer, though depending on your choice of establishment this can vary by a couple of Euros in either direction. Cocktails, 'pints' and wine come more or less at London prices, so while nothing is cheap you shouldn't get too much of a surprise when you get the bill.

copyright qanuk 2004

111

après-ski & nightlife

1. bar d'up
2. chambre neuf
3. cybar/dick's tea-bar/ queen vic
4. expédition
5. goophy
6. jekyll
7. the pub
8. safari
9. south bar
10. la terrasse
11. wild wallabies
12. elevation 1904
13. le privilège
14. le dérapage
15. le garage
16. l'arbate
17. la cantina
18. bpm

avenue du savoy

avenue du mont blanc

l'arve

chamonix süd

chamonix

le moudu

place de l'église

casino

train station

montenvers train station

0   100m   200m

a   b   c   d   e   f

après-ski & nightlife

chambre neuf

☎ 0450 558981
🕐 7am-2am

Perhaps the best (almost certainly the busiest) après bar in Chamonix. It is quite small and not wonderfully designed, but the excellent live music between 5pm and 7pm packs the English and Scandinavian crowds in, and from then there is rarely a lull until it closes. If you want to escape the jam, the terrace is the perfect place to watch the mountains flare pink with the sunset. Its popularity is due to the atmosphere, the homely wooden décor and its location - attached to the hotel Gustavia, it is 2 minutes' walk from the Montenvers train, and the Chamonix Bus stops on the doorstep.

112

the pub

☎ 0450 559288
🕐 4pm-2am

A friendly and busy little place which appeals as much to Chamonix's French contingent as to holiday-makers. It is not a 'cool' bar like many of the places in town - though it can sometimes feel a bit narrow and cramped, it is a fine place to spend an evening away from predictable après revelry. The Pub never gets too rowdy - when it is full it just feels very full. The music is an unpredictable mix of styles - though there is occasionally a live DJ, tunes are normally chosen from the

CDs behind the bar. Live bands at the Pub are rare and a little different to the norm - more likely to be jazz than loud guitars.

bar d'up

☎ 0450 539133
🕐 5pm-2am

At the main-road end of the Rue des Moulins, Bar d'Up pulls off the 'loud music and lots of beer' approach common to many après bars. There is always something going on: regular live bands, late night themed events, Sky Sports for live rugby and football (on very small TVs), a pool table... it is most popular with the early 20s crowd, who are probably least put off by its low-ceilings and slightly boxy feel.

mbc

☎ 0450 536169
🕐 3:30pm-2am

The most welcoming of any of the bars in Chamonix. The only micro-brewery in the valley, with some excellent pression (draught) beers, generously portioned good quality food and bar snacks (including great nachos), beautiful wooden décor, and the "camel" - which would be a giraffe anywhere else - a 3 litre tower of beer with its own tap which is brought your table so you can help yourself. The MBC is a 5 minute walk away from the town centre, so while it is often busy it is rarely filled with drunken hordes - the majority of the crowd is more 'mountain guide' than 'powder virgin'. It is Canadian run, has regular live music in the late afternoon and occasionally a DJ in the evenings, and is very popular with locals and the more discerning of the seasonnaire population.

l'expédition

☎ 0450 535768
🕓 4pm-4am

If Holly Golightly lived in Chamonix, this is where she would go to drink. Slightly more expensive than most other bars - but slightly classier too, without feeling pretentious. One of the few places you'll find flair bar staff, and one of only 2 bars that stays open until 4am. A smallish but well organised space, with comfortable seating and music that isn't all pop. It is another favourite with the locals, and is often busy to the end with those who want to avoid the mass market feel of the clubs. Situated at the end of the Rue des Moulins, it is enough off the drunken track to avoid the crowds.

goophy

☎ 0450 553342
🕓 4pm-2am

Opposite Chambre Neuf and often just as packed, though more of a night haunt than an après bar. It attracts a slightly younger, 'cooler' crowd, and is popular with seasonnaires and locals as well as holidaymakers. Most evenings there is a live DJ - the music is varied and can be a little unusual, but the atmosphere is busy, lively and loud at all times. Contrary to the Chamonix reputation there are often girls in Goophy's - though as likely as not they will have dreadlocks for hair and pro snowboarders for boyfriends. The back section has a good restaurant.

113

south bar

☎ 0450 554307
🕓 7:30-10:30am, 4pm-1:30am

The centre of Cham Sud's social life. The South Bar is run by Swedes, staffed by Swedes and frequented by Swedes - and therefore also by English people looking to meet Swedes. The narrow upstairs gets very crowded after 11pm. Downstairs you'll probably find a little more space, though fewer seats, and the atmosphere is decidedly cosier and more clubby. Regular live bands, local DJs, theme nights (including topless barmen) and proximity to the Garage all contribute to the South Bar's popularity.

après-ski & nightlife

cybar

☎ 0450 536970
🕐 10am-2am

In a lot of ways the heart of Chamonix bar culture. Its diverse attractions include regular events and live music, 4 levels (if you include the Bar des Moulins downstairs), 24 internet stations, a DVD lounge, sofas, a pool table and a large screen for live sport or extreme videos... you can also borrow games like Jenga, Scrabble and chess from behind the bar.

The food is uninspiring, but if you need to eat there are plenty of restaurants outside on the Rue des Moulins. If you need to dance, Dick's is only 20 yards away. The Cybar is a big part of the seasonnaire social scene, and the staff all speak English as a first language so you needn't feel the pressure to bumble through in French.

114

safari

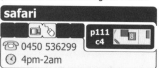

☎ 0450 536299
🕐 4pm-2am

A dark and literally underground bar, which fits a lot into a little space. Odd décor gives it a slightly quirky feel, but it offers everything the larger bars have, just on a smaller scale: a pool table, an internet station, free Playstation 2, and a big TV screen that shows live rugby and football and extreme videos the rest of the time. Safari is also about the cheapest bar in town, and has its own DJ

every night - or if you fancy moving on you can get to the BPM nightclub without having to go outside.

le dérapage

☎ 0450 533641
🕐 4pm-1:30am

A very English hideaway, the Dérapage is an unshowy spot with a genuine welcome. Never too loud, and never too quiet - even if it's empty you'll feel happy just sitting at the bar. No theme nights, no outrageous drinks promotions - it's not a place for the big group pub crawl, partly because it's quite difficult to find, partly because you couldn't fit a big group in the bar anyway. The biggest downside is that the Dérapage could as well be in London or Liverpool - even the most modest GCSE French effort is likely to be lost on the bar staff.

le privilège

☎ 0450 532910
🕐 4pm-2am

New in 2003, the Privilège has filled a surprising niche in the Chamonix après scene. The town's renown for dreadlocks, ice axes and extreme everything has left most bars focussed largely on the party side of post-ski revelry - but the Privilège takes a different tack. It is in almost every way the nicest spot in the valley to sit and relax. The bar at the front is pretty standard and is home to live bands, but round the back or down the stairs you will find all sorts of space and comfy chairs and low lighting and refined décor. If your après brain can see past downing pints, this is very much the place to go.

la terrasse

☎ 0450 530995
🕓 4pm-2am

More expensive, and more up-market than some bars, it is very definitely split between its 2 levels. The downstairs is no different to anywhere else but the first floor has a more refined feel, and the live music and entertainment is more subdued than you would find in places like Wallabies. That said, there is a DJ some nights, and later in the evening it can be just as rowdy as anywhere else.

wild wallabies

☎ 0450 530131
🕓 4pm-2am

A large open plan bar with a bit of everything: sofas, table football, pool, a small dance floor, a restaurant... though nothing out of the ordinary it is lively and loud almost every night of the week. The age range is broader than in some places, and the restaurant is pleasant and quiet in spite of its proximity to the rest of the bar. The music is mostly current pop, Wallabies is a stop on the package trip pub crawls, so don't be surprised to find a large drunken crowd there mid-week.

elevation 1904

☎ 0450 530052
🕓 10am-1:30am

What used to be a quiet spot where middle-aged Frenchmen drank wine all day is now the pretender to the throne of the après scene and the best all-round bar in town. Run by people who know how to run bars, and who also know what music is cool, what food tastes good and how to make a small space feel like somewhere you want to stay all day. You can sit down with a burger and a coke at lunchtime and before you know it it's 9pm and everyone's drinking beer. Whatever the time of day you'll find a warm welcome. Elevation is very much what modern Chamonix is about.

115

queen vic

☎ 0450 531910
🕓 4pm-1:30am

Hemmed in by the Cybar and Dicks, the Queen Vic is a surprising place that doesn't quite fit its name - far from being home to East End grit, and sadly lacking Babara Windsor behind the bar, it is in fact a random mix of low-ceilinged smokiness that is English only by virtue of its clientele. There's pool and plenty of seating, and a couple of cute little cubby-holes which are great if you can get a seat in one. It's the sort of place you'll either like or you won't.

après-ski & nightlife

nightclubs

All but 2 of Chamonix's bars close by 2am, and those not so keen on catching the first lift in the morning head to one of the town's nightclubs. Clubbing in Chamonix is much like in any other ski resort, except perhaps for the broader choice of dancefloors - wherever you are in town there is likely to be a club a short walk away.

Aside from the Garage's curious no-hat policy, you will not encounter a **dress code** anywhere in Chamonix - you are as well off in your ski gear as your party frock, as least as far as the bouncers are concerned.

As with any club in the world, helping out the **boy-girl ratio** won't do your queuing time any harm - crowds of females are pretty rare, and so are highly prized by door staff. When there's no queue, work on getting them to drop the cover charge.

prices

Cover charges vary from place to place, and also depending on what time you arrive, but apart from at the Arbate they're nothing that will trouble your wallet. Cloakrooms also levy a minimal fee - but clubs make their money from drinks prices, which are significantly higher than in the bars.

116

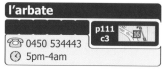

l'arbate

☎ 0450 534443
🕐 5pm-4am

p111
c3

A ski-resort slice of Ibiza nightlife. In case your holiday isn't already costing you enough, you can lose your remaining Euros in Chamonix's only real club - the main weekly night hosts name DJs from across the European club scene, and the blend of skiing euphoria and properly mixed music makes for a wild and memorable experience. It's not for the half-hearted and it's not cheap, but if the weather's bad or you'd rather see the dawn than the rest of the day, the Arbate is your place.

la cantina

☎ 0450 538380
🕐 5pm-2am

p111
f4

A small and out of the way club that is one of the only places that you'll find music that isn't just repetitive commercial dance. La Cantina hosts regular guest DJs championing diverse musical styles - an assortment of reggae, hip-hop, drum and bass, and chill out nights. The best way to find out what's on is to look for the posters around town. There's not much space that isn't dancefloor, but La Cantina regulars are generally more interested in the music than in checking their make-up (or other people's).

dick's tea-bar

☎ 0450 531910
🕙 10pm-4am

The Chamonix branch of Dick's Tea-Bars, made famous by the original in Val d'Isère. A standard fare club with 2 levels and a slightly cramped dancefloor. Nightclub prices too - everything a little more expensive than in the bars - but for that you get the more outgoing of the English tourist and seasonnaire population. There are regular guest DJs, occasional theme nights, and the music is generally what you would expect in any commercial club in England - a bit of everything. The main plus is its location, on the Rue des Moulins, ideal for rounding off a night in the centre of town.

le garage

☎ 0450 536469
🕙 10pm-4am

If you're wondering where the gaggle of Swedes went when they left the South Bar, they're probably at the Garage - the logical progression from any bar in Cham Sud, and the most reliably busy club in town. The owners cleverly employ beautiful Swedish girls to sell their alcohol, so the large bar is always very busy and very male - and people are generally too busy watching their drinks being made to notice the bill when they arrive. Music is nothing out of the ordinary, though the mirrored dancefloor

makes for some entertaining moments watching people watching themselves... the Garage holds regular theme nights - some of which are in questionable taste - and the baguettes on sale in the cloakroom are the only food available in Chamonix at 4am.

bpm

☎ 0450 536352
🕙 10pm-4am

Next to Safari, and the logical progression from the Pub. A surprisingly small bar but a nice enough place, the main attraction of which is the weekly Scandinavian Party - which as the name suggests is intended to bring in lots of English men hoping to meet Swedish girls. Perhaps surprisingly, Scandinavians go too, and the atmosphere tends to be very lively. Music is generally dancey, with the obligatory style changes through hip-hop, cheese and trance.

117

argentière

Though only 7kms down the road, Argentière is a world away from the cosmopolitan bustle that is Chamonix. Smaller in size - basically consisting of 1 long street lined with shops, restaurants and bars - it is big enough to have all that you might need and there is plenty to keep you amused if you have any energy left when you get down off the Grands Montets' moguls.

Most of the shops in the village are dedicated to the plethora of outdoor pursuits on offer in the valley - if you need some crampons you'll be spoilt for choice, but this is not the place to buy your Chanel handbag. Of the rental shops Mont Blanc Sports in the galerie commercial and the Alp Centre are recommended for specialist skiing and mountaineering equipment. For more conventional skis and boots there is a decent branch of the Twinner chain. Otherwise the range of commerce is limited - there are a couple of places for pastries and local produce, but in general the theme is mountainous.

Argentière has the same options as Chamonix for lessons and guiding. The ESF has an Argentière branch (➥ lessons & guiding) - with offices in the town and the Grands Montets cable car building. The guiding company ChamEx is baed in Argentière, as is Evolution 2's Panda Club (➥ children) - there is an Evo2 office in Jorasse Sports just up from the Office Bar. Lift passes

are available from the tourist office and the cable car station. You can buy a lift pass for just Argentière though this is the most expensive of the valley's 4 areas. Even so if you are only staying for a short time and intend to ski only in the Argentière area it remains cheaper to buy it from day to day.

Argentière's smaller size also means that there are fewer restaurants and fewer bars. At least this makes it a lot easier to choose where to eat, and as far as après goes there's a much more defined scene than the sprawl that is Chamonix town. There's enough diversity in the restaurants - the usual mix of Savoyarde and other less French choices - that you should be able to find something you like though there's no truly gourmet food. The choice of drinking holes is more limited - confined to a handful of bars along the strip - and even then what there is tends to double as a restaurant or internet café as well as somewhere to get a 1664. That said, the atmosphere is always friendly and quite lively on certain nights of the week. And should you need more choice of food or drink you can always hop on the bus or into a taxi and head into the big smoke of Chamonix only 10-15 minutes down the road.

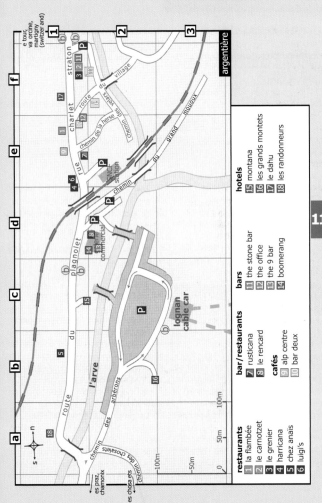

argentière

119

restaurants
1 la flambée
2 le carnotzet
3 le grenier
4 harricana
5 chez anaïs
6 luigi's

bar/restaurants
7 rusticana
8 le rencard

cafés
9 alp centre
10 bar deux

bars
11 the stone bar
12 the office
13 the 9 bar
14 boomerang

hotels
15 montana
16 les grands montets
17 le dahu
18 les randonneurs

<< eating out >>

le grenier £

☎ 0450 540600
🕓 4pm-10pm
🍴 mostly crêpes

Restaurant proof that appearances can be deceptive - though it looks rubbish from the outside, the Grenier is one of Argentière's best eateries. It's basically a simple crêperie serving savoury and sweet varieties, but the food - though fine - is not the reason to go. Like the Bumble Bee on Chamonix's Rue des Moulins it oozes cosy friendliness, and you can't help but relax and enjoy yourself - as long as you like pancakes.

120

harricana £££

☎ 0450 542202
🕓 6pm-10pm
🍴 innovative international

Arguably the best restaurant in Argentière, the Harricana is a cosy and bustling place which advertises itself as having an 'innovative' menu. The adventurous mix of styles will likely inspire curiosity as much as desire, but overall the food is very good and the ambience very pleasant - and there is a regular live pianist to soothe away your aches with a tune or two.

le carnotzet ££

☎ 0450 541943
🕓 4pm-10pm
🍴 traditional savoyarde

Half way up the shabby parade of shops at the top end of town, Le Carnotzet - which effectively translates as a cellar used to entertain friends - is a small and intimate place with a good fondue and some excellent *croûtes* dishes. As with the Grenier, its main draw is that in spite of external appearances, the inside is pleasant and the welcome is warm.

la flambée ££

☎ 0450 541296
🕓 6pm-10pm
🍴 traditional savoyarde

An excellent option for families and groups, La Flambée is a large and bustling all-round restaurant which serves up fondue with a smile. There isn't the widest selection of dishes but if you're looking for melted cheese or chunky steak you could do a lot worse, and you won't balk at the price.

and the rest

If none of this fits the bill, **luigi's** (t 0450 540660) is a very decent Italian restaurant next to Harricana, **chez anaïs** (t 0450 540737) is a slightly quirky local restaurant on the outskirts of the town, or alternatively the restaurant at the **hotel dahu** (t 0450

530448) serves up a respectable evening meal and their terrace is as good a place as any to sit and watch the sun go down.

<< après-ski & nightlife >>

rencard

☎ 0450 541402
🕐 8am-2am

Difficult to pigeon-hole, the Rencard in the galerie commercial is the all day spot for whatever you might fancy - it serves up a hangover curing English breakfast, mixes a stress relieving après vin chaud, and transforms into a pub-style mélange of evening drinking. The subdued lighting makes it a small and cosy place in which everything says 'seasonnaire', from the slightly scruffy décor to the laid-back attitude to the low prices.

bar deux

☎ 0450 541632
🕐 10am-10pm

In the same building as the Office Bar and under the same ownership, Bar Deux is a do-it-all internet café/coffee shop/place to sit on the sofa. There's a Gamecube to keep you amused while you're waiting for a computer, they run a book-swap operation, you can drink beer while you surf the net and rent DVDs for when you leave. It all happens in a

pleasantly relaxed way, and if it's sunny you can lounge with the newspaper on the very small terrace.

rusticana

☎ 0450 540030
🕐 4pm-2am

Run by an Englishman who came for a season and didn't manage to leave, the Rusty is in every way the best that Argentière has to offer. Its portfolio includes welcoming afternoon après and an excellent pseudo-continental food menu ("Toulouse sausages and roast garlic mashed potato"), **121** along with regular live music and lively late night drinking. It's a required stop on the tour, and the sort of place you can go into at 4pm and not feel the need to leave until your bed starts calling.

the 9 bar

☎ 0681 422031
🕐 9pm-2am

Something of a seasonnaire hideaway, the Nine Bar is aimed at a very specific market. There's a small skate pipe in the bar, and - though the dress code is not official - if you forgot to pack your baggy jeans you'd best go shopping before heading here. Music runs along the same lines, as does the party atmosphere, which is young and drunken at the best (or worst) of times.

the office bar

☎ 0450 541632
🕓 8am-10am, 4pm-2am

p119 e1

Refurbished in 2003, the new-style version of the Office has had to work hard to retain its client base. No longer is it in the style of an English pub - blonde wood and purple paintwork abound, and it feels very new and clean and not so smoky as the Office of yore. It opens for breakfast and serves up a decent evening menu, but generally as the name suggests it is a bar. Live music is a regular feature, along with smiling waitresses and Sky TV - and though it is now more French in décor it is still very English in population, and either way it remains one of the best après destinations in Argentière.

122

the stone bar

☎ 0450 541317
🕓 4pm-2am

p119 f1

At the northernmost extent of the commercial strip, the Stone Bar is a good-sized and busy place with a pool table and "all-night happy hour" arrangement. Though perhaps not as good for atmosphere as Rusticana or the Office, it's a change of scene and being at the end of the Argentière strip it can be the first/last stop on any pub crawl you may be planning.

boomerang

☎ -
🕓 4pm-4am

p119 d1

Curiously disguised by the "tapas & sports café" banner, in reality the Boomerang is a nightclub. It's your only choice after 2am, and though they also hold pool competitions, show extreme sports videos and serve tapas, the best time to go is when you can no longer go anywhere else. Guest DJs and a music style that is thankfully not just commercial pop-dance make it a good spot to find the tiles on which to spend your night.

activities

When the lifts are closed because of too little or - more frustratingly - too much snow, there a few things to keep you occupied.

more exercise?
The **centre sportif** Richard Bozon (t 0450 530907, i sports.chamonix.com) has a wide range of facilities - a small but excellent weights room, a solarium, sauna, hammam, a small bouldering wall, tennis and squash courts. The **swimming pool** (centre nautique) is open every day 2pm-8pm, and on Friday evenings until 9pm. One of the indoor pools is 25m long and there is also a jacuzzi, a water slide, and swimming lessons are available. The only problem is the dress code - men are only allowed to swim in speedos. You can pay by the visit for either the centre sportif or nautique.

124

The **tennis** club (t 0450 532840) on Avenue de la Plage has 2 covered courts and 1 squash court, and is open every day 9am-12:15am and 3pm-7:15pm. You can hire rackets if you forgot to pack yours.

The covered and outdoor **ice rinks** (t 0450 531236) are next to the Centre Sportif. The covered rink is open daily 10am-12pm and 3pm-6pm except Wednesday afternoons and 9pm-11pm on Wednesday evenings. The outdoor ice rink is open daily depending on the weather. And if you'd rather watch the experts do it, the indoor ice rink hosts

Chamonix's own **hockey** team, and on occasion the French national team. Games take place on Saturday evenings, and are advertised on banners, posters and fliers.

For exercise at a more leisurely pace the **bowling pub** in Cham Sud (Avenue de Courmayer, t 0450 537437) has 8 lanes, a range of pool and snooker tables, and a bar. It is open daily 5pm-2am (or from 2pm on bad weather days).

Chamonix has **ice climbing** for all levels of ability. It is a good place to start the sport - not least because there are so many willing guides around - but there is also a huge range of challenging ice and mixed routes for the more experienced. Contact any of the guiding companies, though ChamEx are particularly recommended.

Les Houches is home to a superb **indoor climbing centre** - the Mont-Blanc Escalade (t 0450 547648). Anyone whose passion involves ropes and carabiners will be amply satisfied by what's on offer - the place is intimidating both for its routes, which reach 8c+ (French), and for the people who hang out there. If you're very good on a wall - or can get past the initial feeling of utter inferiority - it is a very friendly place to go.

Almost a sport, the arcade at the end of the Rue des Moulins has a **salle des jeux** with a number of more-or-less up

124

to date video games, should you be short on adrenaline and high on expendable cash.

Probably stretching the defintion too far, but you could always exercise your wallet in the **casino** (t 0450 530765). Prominently placed across the road from the Place Sassure, the casino is perhaps best used as a landmark for navigating your way around, but if you have the gambling urge it is open every day from midday until the small hours.

take to the skies
Chamonix Mont-Blanc hélicoptères and SAF Chamonix hélicoptères run daily **panoramic helicopter flights** around the valley - a great way to get a different perspective of the peaks. Chamonix is also the ideal place for **parapenting** (paragliding). The most common launch Le Brévent, alongside the Altitude 2000 chair, though it is also possible to jump from the Aiguille du Midi. The main landing spot is Le Savoy beginners' slope, right in the middle of town. Haut Vol (t 0450 539801/0680 032474) is a parapenting school or the ESF, the Compagnie des Guides, Evo 2, Ski Sensations and Summits all offer tandem jumps.

culture vulture
The **cinema** (programme listings t 0450 530339, bookings t 0450 558998) on Rue Paccard has 3 screens, and usually shows 1 film in English every day - look out for "VO" (*version originale*) on the

schedule. Films run afternoon and evening in much the same way as in England, though there's not much in the way of popcorn or pic n' mix, so if you want to munch you should buy food beforehand. An extra screening is shown on bad weather days.

There is a 2 hour **guided walking tour** of the town on 1 morning every week. Contact the tourist office for more details. If you want a **horse-drawn tour** of the local area, Dr Jivago is your man. He's not very talkative, but travelling through the snow in a carriage is quite enough on its own. It's not cheap, but up to 6 can go at a time. He and his horse are based at the west end of the Avenue Michel Croz.

125

The Musée Alpin, just off the Avenue Michel Croz, is not so much a **museum** of Chamonix as of the surrounding mountains. Permanent exhibits include displays featuring early maps of the area, a history of the attempts to climb Mont Blanc, the story of the development of various winter sports including the first Winter Olympics in 1924, a history of the tourism in the area and a crystal collection. It often has a specialist exhibition, which will be advertised around town. It is open 2pm-7pm and 11am-7pm during school holidays.

The Chamonix valley is well equipped with facilities for children. A few of the tour operators offer day-time childcare and kids clubs, and both the ESF and Evolution 2 offer instruction aimed specifically at young learners. With all facilities for children, you need to book well ahead as spaces are limited - particularly for the ski schools during the school holidays. And a word of caution - children can find it difficult to adapt to the thinner air at high altitude, particularly when coupled with the excitement of places like the Aiguille du Midi, where just the cable car is likely to get their pulse going.

tour operators

Many operators have discounted or free child places in their chalets and some also include free ski and boot hire, lift passes or ski lessons for children. In addition, a few operators run childcare programmes. The forerunner is probably **esprit** - children are a key part of their business - and in Chamonix and Argentière their programme includes everything from a nursery (for children as young as 4 months) to after-ski school care (for children aged 3-12 years). An even greater attraction for some parents will be the evening classes run for 6-12 year olds. Another old-timer for youngsters is **ski hillwood** who specialise in family ski holidays in Argentière and offer a crèche for children aged 6 weeks-3 years as well as an afternoon kids club for 4-11 year olds after ski school.

crystal has a dedicated crèche and nanny service for all children staying in their accommodation, and free evening babysitting in 1 chalet (Chalet Bernadette). **club med**, as you would expect from a leading families operator, has a full day programme for children aged 4-10 years.

in-resort

The tourist office will point you in the direction of qualified **nannies** and **babysitters** - though Chamonix is crawling with seasonnaires in need of Euros, so if you would prefer English-speaking childcare at negotiable rates you won't have to look far. Just ask behind the bar in somewhere like the Cybar or Goophy's.

For a **kindergarten/crèche** the Halte de Garderie (t 0450 53 36 68) on Promenade du Fori will look after children aged 3 months-3 years, while the Maison pour Tous (t 0450 531224) next to the Halte de Garderie organises leisure programmes for children aged 4-11 years.

The ChamSki **lift pass** has a number of options aimed at families and children. Under 16s ('Juniors') and Under 12s ('Kids') get a basic reduction in the price of the pass, and there are also deals on 6-day passes for adult and child combinations. For under 12s who have never skied before, there is a cheaper version of the ChamStart pass, which gives access to the valley-floor lifts.

For **ski lessons** the ESF has 30 specialist children's instructors, and runs lessons for children over the age of 3. Private lessons are the same as for adults, and group lessons in the Kid's Club run at the Savoy slope in Chamonix or in the Jardin d'Enfants in Argentière. Lessons run Mondays-Saturdays, and length varies by the time of the season: from December to the beginning of February they are either 2 or 4 hours long, changing to 2½ or 5 hours from February to the end of the season. There are various different packages on offer, including provision of lunch, child care, and a full 6 day program. Children must wear a helmet to join a group lesson. All the ski rental shops have helmets for hire - though make sure you get one that fits well. Many a tantrum has been thrown because of an ill-fitting helmet.

Evolution 2's Panda Club (t 0450 540476) based in Argentière, runs a schedule of skiing lessons for anyone over the age of 2½ (up to 12), which basically means any child who is a confident walker. Open Sundays-Fridays options include 2 hour and 4 hour lessons, half days (morning or afternoon) and full days, and over Easter the ski lessons combine with a multi-activities programme.

activities

There are events for children throughout the season, including the arrival of Santa Claus in the lead-up to Christmas - as well as the more regular activities listed below. On the snow, the ESF organise a **torch-lit descent** during February and March on Les Grands Montets. Off the snow children under 6 years old can use the **swimming pool** at the Centre Sportif for free. The water garden there is open on Saturdays 10am-11am for children aged 6 months- 4 years. They can also use the bouldering wall, although children under 10 must be accompanied by a guide, and children aged between 10 and 14 must be accompanied by an adult.

eating & drinking
127

Most of Chamonix's restaurants and cafés welcome children, and some offer a childrens menu. **munchie**, **gecko**, and **le pitz** (➜ eating out) are particularly good, as are the restaurants in **wild wallabies** and **goophy** (➜ après-ski & nightlife). Children are also generally allowed into the bars and pubs, and it is up to you whether they drink - nobody is likely to bat an eyelid if a child or teenager drinks wine or has a beer with their parents.

before you go

Before you decide what kind of job you want you need to decide what kind of season you want - a job as a rep will be better paid but you have more responsibility, while a job as a chalet host means fixed hours, but once you know the routine, more time to enjoy resort life. Most of the UK ski companies recruit seasonal workers - from May onwards though there may still be vacancies as late as December. Either contact the companies directly or go through a recruitment website such **natives** (i natives.co.uk) who has a comprehensive database of available jobs as well as a lot of information on everything about "doing a season". It's a competitive market for jobs and while it is not essential, speaking reasonable French will help. If you haven't got a job by October, it's worth going to the Ski Show at Olympia - some tour operators have a stall there as does Natives. If you haven't got a job by the start of the season, it can be worth heading out to the resort (if you can support yourself for a bit). Some of the less glamourous jobs may still be available and you will also get known - so when there is the inevitable fall-out of recruits due to unsuitability, New Year flu and mid-season blues, you can step into the role. Jobs constantly become available throughout the season - the ski market is very transient. Once employed most companies organise your travel to and from the resort, accommodation, lift

pass and equipment rental. Most jobs come with a shared room as part of the 'incentives' package. If accommodation doesn't come with your job or if you aren't planning on having a job you would be well advised to find some digs before you head out. A group of 4 or more should be able to find somewhere that won't break the bank. Single or double apartments are a little harder to come by, and accordingly can be pretty pricey. A very large number of those who work in Chamonix live in lower-priced Les Houches. Some companies specialise in providing accommodation for those planning to stay for a longer period - anything from 2 weeks to the full season. Planet SubZero (i planetsubzero.com) has a range of different options, including a chalet in Argentière, an apartment in the centre of Chamonix, and a more typical seasonnaire spot in Cham Sud.

once you're there

Chamonix has thousands of seasonnaires, and they come from all walks of life. By reputation they all have dreadlocks and baggy pants - but in reality Chamonix's universal draw brings every type of person. There are plenty of hardcore extreme boarders, but they are no means in the majority. Who you wind up befriending depends on 3 things - where you work, where you live, and where you drink. There are so many sub-communities that you won't get to know everyone in the town - which is a welcome relief compared to places like

Val d'Isère or Zermatt where everyone knows everyone else. Another product of the town's size is that it isn't very cliquey. Inevitably some of the bars have their own 'in' crowds, but in general Cham's seasonnaires are more interested in where they are than in being particular about who they're there with. This is true of the nationalities too - though there are oodles of French, Scandinavians and English, Chamonix also brings in Kiwis, Americans, and representatives from any number of other coutries. There isn't really anything to tie the community together. There are plenty of events during the season, but there isn't the 'toga party' student night approach common elsewhere. This isn't to say that Chamonix is any more mature in its approach, just that it's less English dominated. Working in Argentière is a different kettle of fish. As it's a lot smaller. You'll know everyone within a week or two, and you'll have seen closing time in every bar within a similar time period. This is not a problem - you're likely to know someone with a car - and Argentière's community is a very welcoming one. Plus you'll be spending 5 months within walking distance of the Lognan cable car, which means you'll get something most people never will - first tracks on the Grands Montets.

Though every bar is a **hangout** for some seasonnaires, there are a couple of lesser known spots which host more locals than tourists - these will become evident quickly enough if you look, but equally the town is large enough that you could go all season without even hearing of some places. Seasonnaire **prices** are generally unofficial - you're best off getting to know a barman, or being one. Just saying you're a season worker won't cut much mustard with most people. Some of the non-alcohol based places offer discounted rates for those with long term plans. The swiming pool sells passes for 12 visits or on a monthly basis, which works out much cheaper than paying as you go.

Calls home are expensive from an English **mobile**, so it could be worth investing in a French SIM card - generally about £30 (of which £15 is credit) and calls made with in and out of France will be cheaper and you won't pay to receive calls from the UK. Check that your phone is 'unlocked' (so you can insert a foreign SIM card) before you leave the UK. You then pay as you go as you would in the UK. Top up cards are available from the various tabacs and bookshops around town. There are a variety of places to check your **email** - Chamonix has ADSL broadband, and so access is much easier and much faster than in most resorts. The Cybar and Eldorado are the best places to drink coffee as you surf, and there is also a dedicated internet café (emphasis on the 'internet') in the Galerie Blanc Neige (c4). Quite a few of the bars also have 1 or 2 internet stations - and bizarrely McDonald's has 5.

129

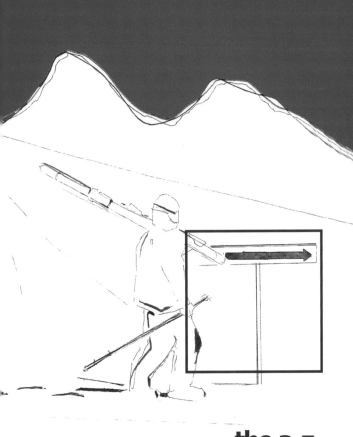

the a-z

tour operators

A list of the English based tour operators offering a range of accommodation in the Chamonix valley. Though many of them offer a variety of different ways to take a skiing holiday they have been categorised according to their main strength.

mainstream
airtours t 0870 238 7777,
i mytravel.com
club med t 0700 2582 932,
i clubmed.co.uk
crystal t 0870 405 5047,
i crystalski.co.uk
equity travel t 01273 886 879,
i equity.co.uk
first choice t 0870 754 3477,
i fcski.co.uk
inghams t 020 8780 4433,
i inghams.co.uk
lagrange holidays t 020 7371 6111,
i lagrange-holidays.co.uk
leisure direction t 020 8324 4042,
i leisuredirection.co.uk
neilson t 0870 333 3356
i neilson.co.uk
thomson t 0870 606 1470,
i thomson-ski.co.uk

ski-specific
french life ski t 0870 197 6692,
i frenchlifeski.co.uk
rocky mountain t 0870 366 5442,
i rockymountain.co.uk
ski activity t 01738 840 888,
i skiactivity.co.uk
ski club of great britain t 020 8410 2022, i skiclub.co.uk

ski independence t 0870 600 1462,
i ski-independence.co.uk
ski wild t 0870 746 9668,
i skiwild.co.uk
ski world t 08702 416723,
i skiworld.ltd.uk

resort-specific
bigfoot t 0870 300 5874, i bigfoot-travel.co.uk
boardnlodge t 020 7916 2275,
i boardnlodge.com
chamactive t 0033 676 220 263,
i chamactive.com
collineige t 0127 624 262,
i collineige.com
concept chalets t 01865 390807,
i conceptchalets.com
high mountain holidays t 0199 377 5540, i highmountain.co.uk
huski t 0207 938 4844, i huski.com
mcnab mountain sports t 0033 450 447 288, i mcnab.co.uk
mountain discovery t 0033 450 447 288,
i mountaindiscovery.co.uk
mountains & molehills t 0138 675 1338,
i alpinechalets.co.uk

children
ski esprit t 01252 618300, i ski-esprit.co.uk
ski hillwood t 01923 290700, i hillwood-holidays.co.uk

self-catering & budget
ams t 01743 340623, i amsrentals.com
skiholidays4less t 01724 290660,
i french-freedom.co.uk
interhome t 020 8891 1294,

tour operators

i interhome.co.uk
into mountains i intomountains.com
uptoyou t 0871 220 3099,
i uptoyou.com

self-drive
drive alive t 0114 292 2971, i drive-alive.com
erna low t 0207 584 2841,
i ernalow.co.uk
eurotunnel motoring holidays t 0870 333 2001, i eurotunnel.com

tailor-made & weekends
alpine weekends t 0208 944 9762,
i alpineweekends.co.uk
flexiski t 0870 909 0754, i flexiski.com
handmade holidays t 01285 648 518,
i handmade-holidays.co.uk
made to measure holidays t 0124 353 3333, i madetomeasureholidays.com
momentum ski t 0207 371 9111,
i momentum.uk.com
ski weekend t 0870 060 0615,
i skiweekend.com
white roc ski weekends t 0207 792 1188, i whiteroc.co.uk

les houches
alps à la carte t 01494 730705,
i alpsalacarte.com
chalet in the mountains t 0041 79242 8478, i chaletinthemountains.com

privately-run
chalet cascade t 0773 098 7600
i chaletcascade.com
chalet chantel 0033 607 502672,
i skiambiance.co.uk

chalet petit tinquer t 0771 1433 758/00 33 667 362143, i chaletpt.com
cham lodge t 0207 373 4013,
i chamlodge.com
chamonix direct t 0033 450 559037,
i chamonix.direct.com
mont blanc lodge t 0033 450 531942,
i montblanclodge.com
snowfalling t 01892 725379,
i snowfalling.com

If you run a ski company that offers holidays to Chamonix but are not listed here, let us know by email to comments@snowmole.com and we will include you in the next edition of this guide.

directory

listings

All 0450 or 06 numbers need the French international prefix (0033) if dialled from the UK. 0826 numbers can only be dialled in France.

Where applicable, references are given to the town map.

transport

air
bmibaby t 0870 264 2229,
i bmibaby.com
british airways t 0870 850 9850,
i ba.com
easyjet t 0870 600 0000,
i easyjet.co.uk
ryanair i ryanair
swiss t 0845 601 0956, i swiss.com
geneva t 0041 22 717 7111,
i gva.ch

car hire
alamo i alamo.com
avis i avis.com
easycar t 0906 333 3333
i easycar.com
europcar i europcar.com
t 0450 536340 (Chamonix, at the BP petrol station (c4))
hertz t 0870 844 8844 i hertz.co.uk

cross-channel
eurotunnel t 0870 535 3535,
i eurotunnel.com
norfolkline t 01304 218400,
i norfolkline.com
speedferries t 01304 203000
i speedferries.com

coach travel
eurolines t 08705 143219,
i nationalexpress.com

driving
general - carry a valid driver's licence, proof of ownership, your insurance

certificate and an emergency triangle.

petrol - petrol stations are few and far between - there are only 3 in the whole valley and none north of Chamonix. They do not open late or have 24-hour self service.

speed limits - in built-up areas the speed limit is 50km/h (unless indicated). The limit is 90km/h on all other roads, 110km/h on toll-free motorways and 130km/h on toll motorways. The last stretch of the Autoroute Blanche to Chamonix is a notorious spot for police speed traps, especially at weekends. Foreign drivers are given spot fines.

signs & rules - motorways in France have blue signs. Most operate a *péage* (toll) system. You must wear a seatbelt in the front and back of a car. Children under 12 must sit in the back and babies and young children must be placed in special baby/young child seats.

traffic info - (recorded) t 0826 022022

helicopter

chamonix mont blanc hélicoptères
t 0450 541382, i cmbh.net

international train

raileurope t 0870 584 8848
i raileurope.co.uk
eurostar t 0870 518 6186
i eurostar.com
TGV i tgv.com

local train

chamonix station t 0450 531394
SNCF t 0892 353535,
i ter-sncf.com/rhone-alpes

maps

All of the libraries sell IGN maps (the French equivalent of the OS).

private bus

alp line t 0677 865282, i alp-line.com
alpine cab i alpinecab.com.
ats t 0709 209 7392, i a-t-s.net
bordercross t 0682 779592,
i bordercross.co.uk
mountain transfers t 07889 942786,
i mountaintransfers.com

public bus

aéroski-bus/sat t 0450 530115
chamonix mont-blanc bus t 0450 530555

directory

health & safety

accidents
If you have an accident on the slopes, you will be taken to the nearest doctor unless you specify a particular one. To confirm you can pay for treatment you will need a credit card and your insurance details. As soon as possible contact your insurance company to check whether they want to arrange your transport home - and ask your doctor for a medical certificate confirming you are fit to travel. If you see an accident on the slopes, tell the nearest rescue centre, usually found at the top or bottom of lifts.

doctors
There are 10 medical practices in Chamonix. The nearest hospital is in Les Favrands, just beyond Chamonix Sud.

emergency numbers
emergency centre/fire brigade t 18 (from a mobile) t 112
gendarmerie (t 0450 530055, Route de la Mollard)
police municipale (t 0450 537502, Rue de L'Hotel-de-Ville)
ambulance t 0450 534620
mountain rescue t 0450 531689
central hospital t 0450 538400
on-call   dentist t 0450 661719
         doctor t 0450 534848
         pharmacy t 0450 533679

health
An E111 form (available from any UK post office) entitles you to treatment under the French health system. While you have to pay for your treatment when you receive it, you can then get a refund for up to 70% of medical expenses - as long as you keep all your receipts.

insurance
It is essential to have personal insurance covering wintersports and the cost of any ambulances, helicopter rescue and emergency repatriation - all these services are very expensive. Insurance policies differ greatly - some exclude off-piste skiing or cover it only if you are with a guide, so you need to check the terms and conditions carefully.

pharmacies
Pharmacie de l'Aiguille du Midi (t 0450 534093) on Avenue de l'Aiguille du Midi, Pharmacie de la Vallée (t 0450 531369) on Rue Joseph Vallot, Pharmacie des Alpes (t 0450 531545) on Rue Paccard and Pharmacie du Mont Blanc (t 0450 531261) on Place de l'Eglise.

safety on the mountain
avalanche danger - the risk of avalanche is graded from 1 to 5.
1 & 2. (yellow) low risk.
3 & 4. (checked yellow and black) moderate risk, caution advised when skiing off-piste
5. (black) high risk, off-piste skiing strongly discouraged.
The risk is displayed on a flag at the main lift stations, but if you are in any

directory

doubt about where it is safe to ski, ask the advice of the lift operators.

food & drink - a skiing holiday is not the time to start a diet. Your body expends energy keeping warm and exercising so it's a good idea to eat a decent breakfast, and carry some chocolate or sweets with you.

The body dehydrates more quickly at altitude and whilst exercising. You need to drink a lot (of water) each day to replace the moisture you lose.

rules of conduct - the International Ski Federation publishes conduct rules for all skiers and boarders:

1. respect - do not endanger or prejudice others.
2. control - ski in control, adapting speed and manner to ability, the conditions and the traffic.
3. choice of route - the uphill skier must choose his route so he does not endanger skiers ahead.
4. overtaking - allowed above or below, right or left, but leave enough room for the overtaken skier.
5. entering & starting a run - look up and down the piste when doing so.
6. stopping on the piste - avoid stopping in narrow places or where visibility is restricted.
7. climbing - keep to the side of the piste when climbing up or down.
8. signs & markings - respect these.
9. assistance - every skier must assist at accidents.
10. identification - all involved in an accident (including witnesses) must exchange details.

snow & avalanche information

t 0892 681020

weather

The Office de Haute Montagne in the Maison de la Montagne (e4) has live weather reports or call t 0892 700330 (recorded information in English, updated daily) or log on to meteo.fr

what to wear

Several, thin layers are better than one thick piece. Avoid cotton, which keeps moisture next to the body, so cooling it down. A windproof and waterproof material (such as Goretex) is best for outer layers. A hat is essential to keep you warm and protect the scalp from sunburn as are gloves to keep hands warm. Sunglasses or goggles are essential. Wrap-arounds are a good choice and lenses should be shatter-proof and give 100% protection from UVA and UVB rays. Poor eye protection can lead to snowblindness, which makes the eyes water and feel painful and gritty. Treat by resting eyes in a darkened room, and applying cold compresses. You should wear UVA and UVB sun protection with a high factor (SPF) at all times, even if overcast and cloudy. The sun is more intense at higher altitude, so you should re-apply regularly (particularly after falling or sweating). Don't forget to cover your ear lobes and the underside of the nose.

directory

resort survival

banks & atms
Banque Laydernier and Banque de Savoie on Place Balmat open Mondays-Fridays 9am-12pm and 3pm-6pm. All have 24 hour ATMs, but plan ahead if you want money at weekends as they can run out.

carte d'hôte
If you are staying in a hotel, you should receive one when you arrive. The card gives you reductions for some public facilities including parking and the Centre Sportif.

church services
The église Saint-Michel (e4) holds Catholic services in French at 6:30pm on Saturdays and 10:30am and 6pm on Sundays. A Protestant service is held at 24 Passage du Temple on the 1st and 3rd Sundays in December, January, March and April at 10am and every Sunday at 10am in February.

dvds & videos
There is a rental shop on the road behind the Brioche'In (f4) and one on the Avenue de L'Aiguille du Midi in Chamonix Sud (c3).

internet/email
The main internet centre is the Cybar (f3), which has 24 stations. There is an internet café is in the Galerie Blanc Neige (c4), where you can buy credit - there is also a 24 hour terminal outside.

Lots of bars have 1 or more stations: Eldorado has 5, as does Mcdonalds. Chambre Neuf and Safari each have 1, and there is 1 in the Galerie Alpina (f3). In Argentière there is a terminal in the Galerie Commerciale and in the Office. All the terminals are inexpensive and prices are similar, with an initial charge and then a per minute addition.

laundry & dry cleaning
Laverie du Mont Blanc on the Avenue de l'Aiguille du Midi and Pressing de l'Arve in the Galerie Alpina.

library
Open (t 0450 533482) 2:30pm-6:30pm Tuesdays-Saturdays and 9am-12pm on Wednesdays.

lift pass company
compagnie du mont blanc
(t/f 0450 531414/9244)

market
Chamonix is a market town, and on Saturday mornings the car park next to the Alpina hotel is taken over by stalls selling local produce.

massages
When it all gets too much plenty of places offer body-restoring massages. Anne de Sampigny, t 0680 961352, Le Bachal t 0450 530509, Institut Apparence t 0450 531145, Institut de Beauté Mixte Apollon & Messaline t 0450 534231 and Nikki Jennings t 0638 736351 (home visits).

directory

newspapers
Some of the libraries stock a small selection of English newspapers, or you can read them in the Cybar.

parking
Parking on the roads is allowed where indicated - in town there are many pay & display spaces along the roads, all of which are free over lunchtime. At weekends the car parks become very busy.

passport photos
There are photo booths in the tourist office (e4) and at the SNCF Train Station (e1).

post
The post office (t 0450 531590) on the Place Balmat (e3) opens Mondays-Fridays 8:30am-12pm and 2pm-6pm and Saturdays 8am-12pm.

radio stations
Fun Radio 94.9FM
Radio Mont Blanc 89.2FM
NRJ 100.4FM
Couleur 3 99.9FM

shopping
Most shops open every day (except public holidays) 8:30am-12:30pm and 2:30pm-7pm.
supermarkets - Chamonix has 5 - the Marché U (f4), a Grand Casino (b3) and 3 Petit Casinos.
bread - there are any number of boulangeries in town. The best is Le Petrin on the Place du Mont-Blanc (f2).
cheese - is best bought from the supermarket, if you can stand the queues. Places like the Refuge Payot and Alpage des Aiguilles sell good quality cheeses but at somewhat inflated prices.
wine - as with cheeses, the best wines are available away from the tourist traps. The Comptoir du Caviste (f/g4) has an excellent and well priced selection along with knowledgeable and friendly ownership, and the Caves Ribeyrolles (f1) is a huge wine warehouse.
clothes - the larger ski shops stock most outdoor brands, in addition to which there are outlet stores for Helly Hansen, Patagonia, Quiksilver and Rip Curl. All are situated on Rue du Docteur Paccard.

ski & board servicing
WWS, a specialist servicing shop, is next to Cappadoce in Cham Sud.

tourist offices
chamonix - the tourist office (t/f 0450 530024/5890, i chamonix.com) is opposite the Maison de la Montagne (e4) and opens Mondays-Sundays 8:30am-12:30pm and 2pm-6pm and on Saturdays and Sundays of the Christmas and February holidays 8:30pm-7pm. Most information is free and available in English.
argentière - the tourist office (t/f 0450 540214/0639, i argentiere.com) is on Route du Village

(f2) and opens Mondays-Sundays
8:30am-12pm and 3pm-7pm.

wcs

There are public toilets by the tourist
office and at each valley floor lift
station.

websites

There are any number of Chamonix
websites, which give information of
varying degrees of accuracy. One of the
best and the most comprehensive is
chamonet.com For up-to-date details of
weather and lift closures,
compagniedumontblanc.fr is the best
site and is easily navigable even if your
French isn't great.

directory

country survival

customs
As France is part of the EU, there are few restrictions on what UK visitors can take out for personal use.

electricity
220 volts/50hz ac. Appliances use a 2-pin plug - adaptors are readily available from mr bricolage on the edge of cham sud, other electrical stores or supermarkets.

language
English is widely spoken, though an attempt at French is widely appreciated.

money
The currency is the Euro (€). €1 is equivalent to 100 centimes. Notes come in anything from €10 to €500. You can exchange money in all the banks in Chamonix during the week, and also at Geneva airport and in major train stations. There is a bureau de change on Rue de la Gare (e2) and one on Place Balmat (e3) for currency exchange 7 days a week. In 2004, the average exchange rate for UK£1 = (approx) €1.6

public holidays
December 6 - St Nicholas Day
25 - Christmas Day
26 - St Stephen's day
January 1 - New Year's Day
March/April Good Friday, Easter Sunday & Monday

telephone
Public phones boxes are located throughout the town and accept coins or phonecards, which can be bought from the post office, tabacs, and train and petrol stations. All local and calls within Europe are cheaper 7pm-8am during the week and all day at the weekend. The international dialling code for France is 0033; the free international operator t 12; the international directory information t 1159; and national directory information t 111. There are 3 mobile phone networks: Bouyges Telecom, France telecom/Orange and SFR.

time
France is always one hour ahead of England.

tipping
All food bills include a service charge, though it is common to make an addition for drinks or for noticeably good service.

water
Tap water is drinkable, except where there is an eau non potable sign.

glossary

arête - a sharp ridge.

avalanche - a rapid slide of snow down a slope.

avalanche transceiver - a device used when skiing off-piste, which can both emit and track a high frequency signal to allow skiers lost in an avalanche or a crevasse to be found.

BASI - British Association of Snowsport Instructors.

binding - attaches boot to ski.

black run/piste - difficult, generally steeper than a red piste.

blood wagon - a stretcher on runners used by ski patrollers to carry injured skiers off the mountain.

blue run/piste - easy, generally wide with a gentle slope.

bubble → 'gondola'.

button (or Poma) lift - for 1 person. Skis and boards run along the ground, whilst you sit on a small 'button' shaped seat.

cable car - a large box-shaped lift, running on a thick cable over pylons high above the ground, which carry up to 250 people per car.

carving - a recently developed turning technique used by skiers and boarders to make big, sweeping turns across the piste.

carving skis - shorter and fatter than traditional skis, used for carving turns.

chairlift - like a small and uncomfortable sofa, which scoops you and your skis off the ground and carries you up the mountain. Once on, a protective bar with a rest for your skis holds you in place. Can carry 2-6 people.

couloir - a 'corridor' between 2 ridges, normally steep and narrow.

crampons - spiked fittings attached to outdoor or ski boots to climb mountains or walk on ice.

draglift or (T-bar) - for 2 people. Skis and boards run on the ground, whilst you lean against a small bar.

drop-off - a sharp increase in gradient.

edge - the metal ridge on the border of each side of the ski.

FIS - Federation Internationale du Ski.

flat light - lack of contrast caused by shadow or cloud, making it very difficult to judge depth and distance.

freeriding, freeskiing - off-piste skiing.

freestyle - skiing involving jumps.

glacier - a slow-moving ice mass formed thousands of years ago and fed each year by fresh snow.

gondola (or bubble) - an enclosed lift, often with seats.

heliskiing - off-piste skiing on routes only accessible by helicopter.

high season - weeks when the resort is (generally) at full capacity.

itinerary route (yellow) - not groomed, maintained or patrolled.

glossary

Generally more difficult, at least in part, than a black piste. Can be skied without a guide.

k
kicker - jump.

l
lambchop drag → 'rope tow'.

ledgy - off-piste conditions in which there are many short, sharp drop-offs.

low season - beginning and end of the season and the least popular weeks in mid-January.

m
mid season - reasonably popular weeks in which the resort is busy but not full.

mogul - a bump, small or large, on or off piste. A large mogulled area is called a mogul field.

o
off-piste - the area away from marked, prepared and patrolled pistes.

p
parallel turn - skis turn in parallel.

piste - a ski run marked, groomed and patrolled, and graded in terms of difficulty (blue, red or black).

piste basher - a bulldozer designed to groom pistes by smoothing snow.

pisteur - a ski piste patroller.

Poma → 'button lift'.

powder - fresh, unbashed or untracked snow.

r
raquettes → 'snowshoes'.

red run/piste - intermediate, normally steeper than a blue piste, although a flatish piste may be a red because it is narrow, has a steep drop-off or because

snow conditions are worse than on other pistes.

rope tow (or lambchop drag) - a constantly moving loop of rope with small handles to grab onto to take you up a slope.

s
schuss - a straight slope down which you can ski very fast.

seasonnaire - an individual who lives (and usually works) in a ski resort for the season.

skis - technology has changed in the last 10 years. New skis are now shorter and wider. When renting, you will be given a pair approx. 5-10cms shorter than your height.

ski patrol - a team of piste patrollers

skins - artificial fur attached to ski base, for ski touring.

snow-chains - chains attached to car tyres so that it can be driven (cautiously) over snow or ice.

snowshoes - footwear resembling tennis rackets which attach to shoes, for walking on soft snow.

spring snow - granular, heavy snow conditions common in late season (when daytime temperatures rise causing snow to thaw and re-freeze).

steeps - a slope with a very steep gradient.

t
T-bar → 'draglift'.

w
white-out - complete lack of visibility caused by enveloping cloud cover.

index

144

index

also available...

the snowmole guides to

courchevel les 3 vallées
including 1850, 1650, 1550,
le praz & la tania and full
coverage of the 3 vallées
ski area ...

les arcs paradiski
including peisey-vallandry
& arc 1950 and full coverage
of the paradiski area and the
vanoise express...

la plagne paradiski
including all 10 resorts and full
coverage of the paradiski area and
the vanoise express...

méribel les 3 vallées
including méribel centre, les
allues, méribel village & mottaret
and full coverage of the 3 vallées
ski area...

also available...

val d'isère espace killy
including st. foy and
full coverage of the espace
killy area...

verbier val de bagnes
including full coverage of the
4 vallées from verbier to
veysonnaz...

zermatt matterhorn
including full coverage of the
zermatt-cervinia ski area and the
matterhorn

and coming soon the snowmole guides to...

st. anton arlberg
tignes espace killy
ski weekends
alpine secrets

& also the underground network

further information

accuracy & updates

We have tried our best to ensure that all the information included is accurate at the date of publication. However, because places change - improve, get worse, or even close - you may find things different when you get there. Also, everybody's experience is different and you may not agree with our opinion. You can help us, in 2 ways: by letting us know of any changes you notice and by telling us what you think - good or bad - about what we've written. If you have any comments, ideas or suggestions, please write to us at: snowmole, 45 Mysore Road, London, SW11 5RY or send an email to comments@snowmole.com

snowmole.com

Our website is intended as a compliment to our guides. Constantly evolving and frequently updated with news, you will find links to other wintersport related websites, information on our stockists and offers and the latest news about future editions and new titles. We also use our website to let you know of any major changes that occur after we publish the guides. If you would like to receive news and updates about our books by email, please register your details at www.snowmole.com

order form

The snowmole guides are available from all major bookshops, wintersports retailers or direct from Qanuk Publishing & Design Ltd. To experience the Alps without leaving home have your next snowmole guide delivered to your door. To order send an email to sales@snowmole.com or fill in the form below and send it to us at Qanuk Publishing & Design Ltd, 45 Mysore Road, London, SW11 5RY

the snowmole guide to:	ISBN	quantity
chamonix mont blanc	0-9545739-3-5	
courchevel les 3 vallées	0-9545739-5-1	
la plagne paradiski	0-9545739-8-6	
les arcs paradiski	0-9545739-7-8	
méribel les 3 vallées	0-9545739-4-3	
val d'isère espace killy	0-9545739-9-4	
verbier val de bagnes	0-9545739-2-7	
zermatt matterhorn	0-9545739-6-X	

total: ------------------------------
(£6.99 each, postage & packaging free)

I enclose a cheque for £
(made payable to Qanuk Publishing & Design Ltd)

name --
address ---
postcode --
tel --
email address ---
(please use block capitals)

Delivery will normally be within 14 working days. The availability and published prices quoted are correct at the time of going to press but are subject to alteration without prior notice. Please note that this service is only available in the UK.

Qanuk would like to keep you updated on new titles in the snowmole range or special offers. If you do not wish to receive such information please tick here ☐
Qanuk has a number of partners in the ski industry, and we may from time to time share your details with those partners if we think it might be of interest to you. If you do not wish us to share your details please tick here ☐

about you

Your comments, opinions and recommendations are very important to us. To help us improve the snowmole guides, please take a few minutes to complete this short questionnaire. Once completed please send it to us at Qanuk Publishing & Design Ltd.

name (Mr/Mrs/Ms) --
address --
postcode ---
email address ---
age --
occupation --

1. about your ski holiday (circle as appropriate)
how many days do you ski each year?
weekend/1 week/2 weeks/1 month/more
when do you book?
last-minute/1 month before/1-3 months before/3-6 months before/6+months before
how do you book your holiday?
travel agent/mainstream tour operator/ski-specific tour operator/diy

2. about the snowmole guide
which title did you buy? --
where and when did you buy it? ---
have you bought any other snowmole guides? --
if so, which one(s) ---
how would you rate each section out of 5 (1 = useless, 5 = very useful)
getting started ---
the skiing --
the resort --
the directory --
the maps ---
what in particular made you buy this guide? --
----
do you have any general comments or suggestions? ---------------------------------------
----
did you buy any other guides for your holiday? --
if yes, which one? --
Qanuk Publishing & Design Ltd may use information about you to provide you with details of other products and services, by telephone, email or in writing. If you do not wish to receive such details please tick here ☐

about us

snowmole / snōmōl / n. & v. **1** a spy operating within alpine territory (esp. ski resorts) for the purpose of gathering local knowledge. **2** (in full **snowmole guide**) the guidebook containing information so gathered. v. research or compile process intelligence on an alpine resort or surrounding mountainous area.

the authors

Isobel Rostron and Michael Kayson are snowsport enthusiasts who met while taking time out from real life to indulge their passion - Isobel to get it out of her system and Michael to ingrain it further. Michael's approach having won, they decided that a return to real life was overrated and came up with a cunning plan to make their passion their work. The result was snowmole.

acknowledgments & credits

None of this would have been possible without the help and support of many people:

Laure Châtelard (Office de Tourisme de Chamonix), Helen & Simon Brotherton for their generous hospitality, Steph Lightfoot, Sarah Gilbertson, Jim Scannel, Jo & Victor, Simon & Amy, Wendy Stephenson, Lotta, Andrew Lilley for his invaluable and underpaid proofreading skills, Angela Horne, Julian Horne, Maisie, Christine & Peter Rostron and Henry, Katie & Tom Fyson for their ongoing support.

The publishers would like to thank the following for their kind permission to reproduce their photographs.

back cover: Office de Tourisme de Courchevel 1850 & Office de Tourisme de La Tagne
guide: all pages (except page 89) Office de Tourisme de Chamonix, page 89 Nigel Finch

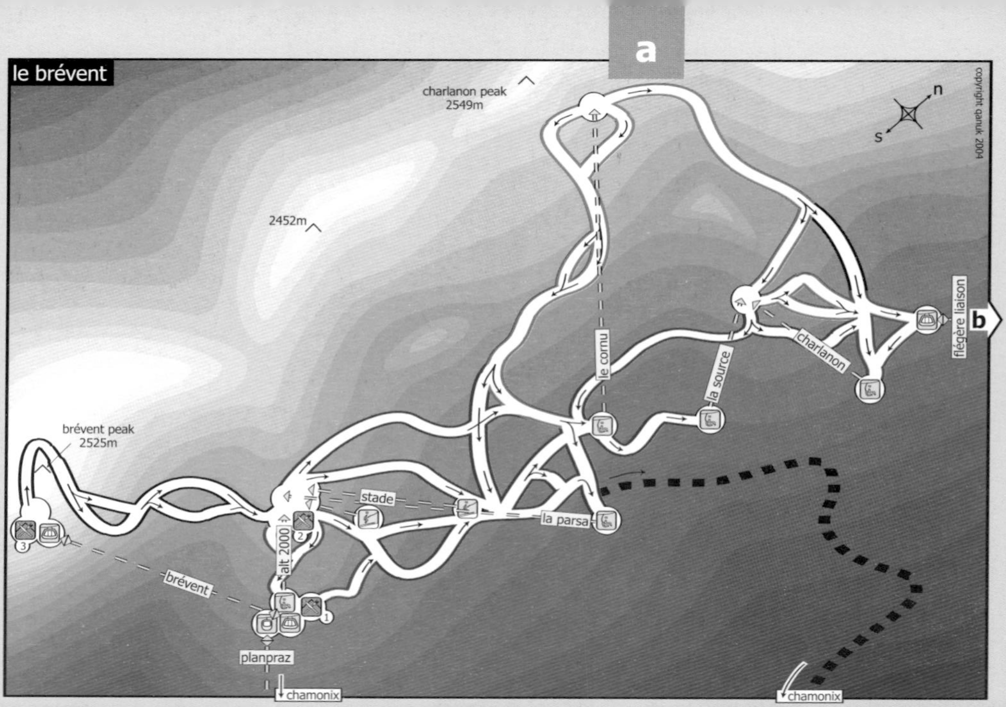

le brévent

copyright qanuk 2004

flégère liaison

charlanon

la source

le cornu

la parsa

stade

alt 2000

chamonix

planpraz

brévent

charlanon peak
2549m

2452m

brévent peak
2525m

chamonix

le brévent

le brévent		pistes	queues	moguls I II III IIII	off-piste I II III IIII
planpraz	6 10m40		⚔⚔⚔ 🕐		●
altitude 2000	2 2m50	■	⚔⚔⚔		●
brévent	60 3m30	■			
stade	1 4m50	■ ■	⚔⚔⚔⚔		● ●
la parsa	4 7m20	■ ■	⚔⚔⚔⚔		● ●
le cornu	3 9m20	■ ■	⚔⚔⚔⚔	●	● ●
la source	4 3m10	■ ■			● ●
charlanon	4 3m40	■	⚔		●
flégère liaison	40 2m45		⚔		

1 altitude 2000
2 la bergerie
3 le panoramic

i	
altitude 2000	avoid the queue by hiking past the bergerie restaurant to join the piste lower down
stade	téléski difficile
la parsa	avoid the queue by taking the stade draglift
la source	this is the fastest route to the flégère

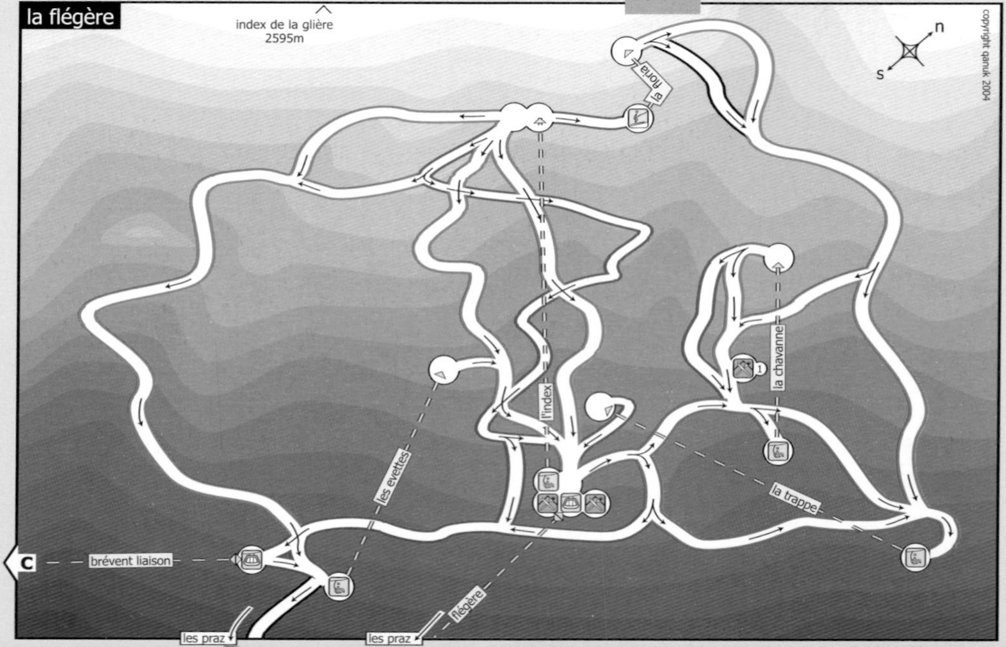

la flégère

index de la glière
2595m

b

copyright qanuk 2004

n
s

la floria

la chavanne

la trappe

l'index

les evettes

la flégère

les praz

les praz

brévent liaison

c

la flégère

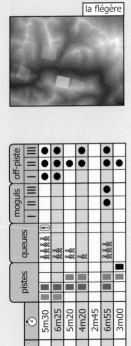

la flégère

	⏱	pistes	queues	moguls I	II	III	off-piste I	II	III
i flégère	60	5m30	▪▪	🚡🚡🚡🚡🚡 ⛷				●	●	●
i la trappe	4	6m25	▪▪	🚡🚡🚡				●	●	● ●
la chavanne	3	5m20	▪ ▪	🚡🚡🚡 ⛷					●	●
les evettes	3	4m20	▪ ▪	⛷						●
brévent liaison	40	2m45	▪			●	●			
l'index	3	6m55	▪	🚡🚡🚡		●	●		●	
i la floria	1	3m00	▪■						●	●

i	
flégère	often closes in high winds
la trappe	slow and often stopped
la floria	leads to runs that are sheltered from the wind

1 la chavanne

b

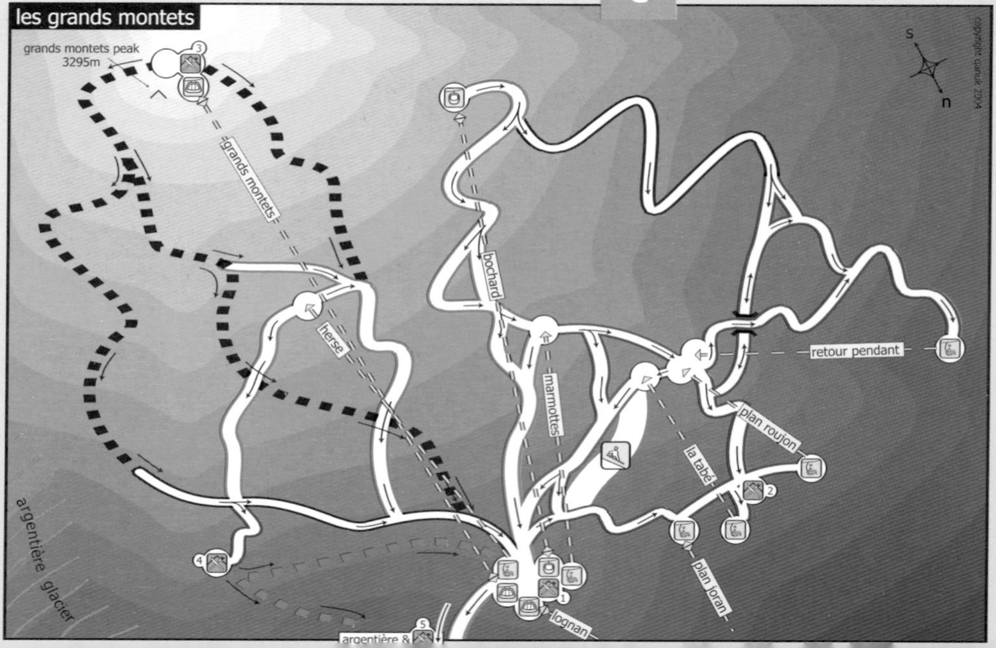

les grands montets

grands montets peak
3295m

C

copyright manuk 2004

retour pendant

plan roujon

la tabé

plan joran

marmottes

bochard

lognan

argentière &

herse

grands montets

argentière glacier

les grands montets

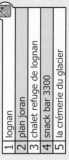

les grands montets

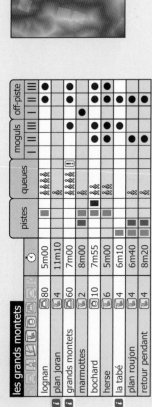

		⏱	pistes	queues	moguls I	II	III	off-piste I	II	III
lognan	80	5m00		❄❄❄				●	●	
i plan joran	4	11m10		❄				●		
i grands montets	60	7m00		❄❄❄ ▯				●	●	
marmottes	2	8m00		❄		●			●	
bochard	10	7m55		❄❄		●		●	●	
herse	6	5m00		❄	●				●	
i la tabé	4	6m10		❄						
plan roujon	4	6m40		❄		●				
retour pendant	4	8m20		❄		●				

i

plan joran	alternative route up/down from the base station
grands montets	ticket required for each journey (available at the mid-station)
la tabé	snowpark access

1 lognan
2 plan joran
3 chalet refuge de lognan
4 snack bar 3300
5 la crémerie du glacier

C

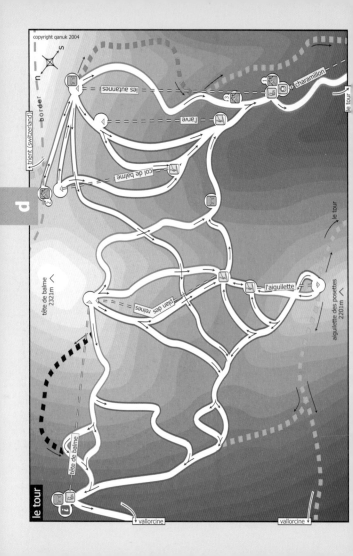

copyright qanuk 2004

le tour

d

tête de balme
2321m ⋀

aiguilette des posettes
2201m ⋀

border

trient (switzerland)

les autannes

l'arve

col de balme

plan des reines

l'aiguilette

le tour

charamillon

le tour

tête de balme

vallorcine

vallorcine

le tour

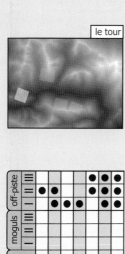

le tour

	🕐	pistes	queues	moguls I II III IIII	off-piste I II III IIII
charamillon	6	8m20			
les autannes	4	7m00			
l'arve	1	4m10			
col de balme	1	4m40			
l'aiguilette	1	3m50			
plan des reines	1	6m15			
tête de balme	4	7m40			

autannes	very cold when windy
col de balme	a short hike from the top to the col de balme refuge hut
aiguilette	leads to a number of itinerary routes
tête de balme	a new lift is planned linking le tour to vallorcine

⭘ ski area key

a - le brévent
b - la flégère
c - les grands montets
d - le tour

the circle indicates the page orientation
of the individual ski maps – the arrow
points towards the top of the page